UNDERGROUND WALES

Trevithick's Tunnel, Merthyr Tydfil.

UNDERGROUND WALES

MARTYN FARR

GOMER

First impression—2001

Hardback ISBN 1 84323 036 4
Softback ISBN 1 85902 933 7

Printed in Wales at
Gomer Press, Llandysul, Ceredigion

Contents

ACKNOWLEDGEMENTS

I never cease to be amazed at the kindness and generosity displayed by so many people when asked for help, and I am conscious that I have required a lot in the compilation of *Underground Wales*!

First and foremost, I am extremely indebted to my photographic assistants, for without their skill, patience and good humour the photographs simply would not be available. Pat Cronin, Phil Dotchon, Richard Hill, Jennifer Pinder and my good friend the late Peter Fowler have been true bastions of support and encouragement throughout. To you and the many others who have suffered the discomforts of underground photography, please accept my humble thanks.

I also thank those people who have given so freely of advice when selecting the sites for inclusion and have loaned books and other research material. To the following I express my sincere gratitude but dissociate them from any errors of fact or interpretation of which I may be guilty: Nigel Burns, Pat Cronin, Jan Langmead, John Parker, Huw Rees and Dyfed Elis-Gruffydd.

For reading the text and for offering positive comment and criticism, I thank Pat Cronin and Richard Hill. Finally, for help with computer technology, production of maps and diagrams, and for regularly repairing various items of photographic equipment I am deeply indebted to Phil Dotchon. Thank you all.

Martyn Farr

FOREWORD

Few of us venture underground. Caves, such as Dan yr Ogof in the Swansea valley, and sites such as Dinorwig Power Station, at Llanberis, may well be places that tourists will frequent in considerable numbers. However, this belies the true extent of a world that few will ever see. Below the surface of the land there are powerful raging rivers, caverns as big as football stadiums, and tunnels wider than a motorway. Within these caves and mines there are fantastic sights: strange sculptures and wonderful rock formations, scenery every bit as interesting and beautiful as anything found on the surface.

This underworld instils a sense of excitement in all who enter, be they casual tourists wandering through a show-cave or mine, or true sporting enthusiasts combating all that nature can present. Caves are dark and mysterious, and few have been completely explored even today. Mines can be equally challenging and

provide an altogether different insight into our nation's rich and varied past. We can learn much from this subterranean world: of geology, hydrology, biology, archaeology, history, and indeed about ourselves.

I hope that the images in this book will stir your imagination and serve, in some small measure to communicate both the enchantment and wonder of the subterranean world, and the pressing need for its long-term conservation. This is a book with a strong photographic bias. Consequently, historical and technical information is necessarily brief and the reader is referred to the bibliography at the back of the volume in order to pursue areas of interest. Again, given the large number of sites that fall within the scope of this publication, the author has been required to be particularly selective with his subject matter. He apologies at the outset for omissions.

Introduction

Wales is renowned for its majestic scenery, its wild and rugged mountains and its beautiful coastline. The three National Parks – Snowdonia, the Brecon Beacons, and the Pembrokeshire Coast – are living testimony to the quality of the landscape. Each reflects a different aspect of the nation's geography: bleak and rocky mountains in the north; the rounded, more subdued topography in the south; and spectacular coastal scenery in the west.

To the visitor the landscape is often the major attraction. But many will not fully appreciate that there is far more to this rich and varied country. Geologically, Wales is as rich as any nation on Earth. The various rocks have generated immense mineral wealth over the years; it is no coincidence that the industrial revolution of the nineteenth century was driven in large measure by the raw materials obtained in Wales. In the early 1800s, for example, Merthyr Tydfil was the iron-making capital of the world. Iron, and certainly coal, not only led to the development of the characteristic terraced housing and ribbon-like communities of the South Wales valleys but also to the rise of Cardiff, Newport and Swansea, which grew to prominence as ports exporting the mineral wealth.

It is also worth noting that even earlier, in the seventeenth century, the Cardigan-shire lead and zinc field was the largest in the world and as a result of this activity we have been left with a legacy of over 7,000 holes, shafts and horizontally-driven tunnels or 'adits'. Only about 1,000 of these are accessible today. Likewise, we must not forget the gold won from places such as Dolaucothi, near Pumsaint and the copper which was obtained from sites such as the Great Orme at Llandudno and Parys Mountain on Anglesey.

In North Wales it was slate that figured most prominently and the vast amount of waste material strewn upon the surface in places such as Blaenau Ffestiniog gives a clear indication as to the magnitude of the industry.

Limestone, formerly of importance in the iron-making industry, today supplies the essential materials for road-building and construction purposes generally. This is found in a narrow belt which surrounds the South Wales coalfield and, to a more limited extent, adjacent to the coalfield of north-east Wales. Silica deposits, used to fabricate refractory bricks and to line the walls of blast furnaces, were also exploited in the same vicinity.

Some of the mineral wealth has been exploited throughout recorded history but much has been sporadic or episodic. Limestone extraction and lime burning is typical of the way a small 'cottage' industry has been transformed. The slate industry, and coal mining, has undergone a similar transformation, rising to supremacy in the late nineteenth century and declining markedly in the early years of the twentieth century. What many people often fail to appreciate is that when these industries were at their height tens of thousands were employed and a substantial proportion of these worked underground.

For miners the hours were long. During the winter months they would descend before dawn and toil until well after dark, six days a week. Much of the work was extremely physical in nature and the working conditions were often very dangerous. In the coalmines there was the ever-present risk of explosion due to the escape of methane gas or 'firedamp'. And there were added dangers, in particular the insidious ailment that affected the lungs. Commonly referred to as 'dust', or 'miner's lung' (medically described as silicosis and pneumoconiosis) the affliction was as crippling and incapacitating as any long-term physical injury.

It also surprises many people today to learn of the extent of these mines and caverns, which were driven to great depths and tens of kilometres in length. Some of the slate mines near Blaenau Ffestiniog, for example, contain over 60 kilometres of passageways, while the lead mines and associated workings beneath Halkyn Mountain, near Mold, may well extend to 80 kilometres or more. The complex network of tunnels connecting some of the coalmines of South Wales would have run to hundreds of kilometres.

Some amazing sights are to be found in these abandoned mines: huge caverns and all manner of interesting artefacts. A visit to a site such as Llechwedd Slate Caverns, Blaenau Ffestiniog (SH 708471) cannot fail to impress the visitor for here, he or she will encounter kilometre after kilometre of vast caverns hewn from the rock by the most elemental techniques imaginable. Mine exploration clearly represents an inviting challenge and gives a wholly unique insight into our nation's rich and varied history.

The natural world of caves is every bit as exciting and visually stunning. Caves may be found in a variety of rocks, including fissures in coastal cliffs. Sea caves are generally short, and relatively few extend beyond the light of day. Those found inland, however, primarily in areas of limestone rock, are altogether more extensive and few have been completely explored even today.

FOLKLORE, MYTH & LEGEND

Man's interaction with the underground world has always been fascinating. In myth and legend, many stories are centred upon caves. Some caves supposedly lead to Hell; others are said to be the repository of hidden treasures, whilst yet others are places where fugitives have sought refuge.

There are several caves in Wales associated with King Arthur. One such lies in a yet-to-be-discovered cave in the vicinity of Craig y Dinas, near Pontneddfechan. Here, folklore would have us believe that Arthur lies sleeping in a vast cavern surrounded by Knights of the Round Table, and a not inconsiderable amount of treasure, awaiting the day when he will be called forth to save the nation from some terrible calamity. Another tale relates to a cave which is supposed to exist in the forbidding cliffs of Lliwedd, near the summit of Snowdon, while yet another speaks of Arthur's treasure, which is said to be buried in a cave at Llangwyfan on Anglesey. Arthur's trusty magician, Merlin, is sometimes said to be imprisoned in a cave on Myrddin's Hill, near Carmarthen.

Mythical dragons were often given the responsibility of guarding treasures in subterranean caverns. Even as late as the nineteenth century certain country folk firmly believed in the existence of these winged serpents, the most infamous of which frequented the deep gorges at the head of the Vale of Neath. It is more than tempting to ascribe their abode to places such as the deep and spacious caves of Cwm Pwll y Rhyd (SN 911137) and Porth yr Ogof (SN 928124).

The Welsh hero, Owain Lawgoch (Owain of the Red Hand) – one of the last chieftains to fight against the English – is reputed to sleep in a cave beneath Carreg Cennen castle (SN 668191). Twm Siôn

Cati, a sixteenth-century Welsh version of the outlaw Robin Hood, was said to have taken advantage of a 'cave' or rock shelter (SN 782467) in the heavily wooded crags of the Tywi valley, between Llandovery and Llyn Brianne reservoir. This particular retreat is well concealed and it is probable that Twm (his real name was Thomas Jones) managed to evade the local sheriff for quite some time! Another isolated rock shelter, 500 metres south-east of Aberedw, near Builth, is known locally as Ogof Llywelyn (SO 084469). This site measures a very comfortable three metres by two metres and is believed to be one of the places where Llywelyn, the last native Prince of Wales, went into hiding following his defeat by the English.

Carreg Cennen castle, Trapp.

Ogof Twm Siôn Cati,
near Rhandir-mwyn.

Reynard's Cave, St Donat's.

Apart from the wildly exaggerated tales of various dogs and birds that have disappeared into particular caves and then reappeared many miles away, there are curious tales vaguely reminiscent of the legendary 'Pied Piper of Hamlyn'. One such concerns a cave near Llanymynech, near Oswestry, close to the English border. Here, apparently, a young harpist discovered that a cave led beneath Llanymynech church. He then laid a wager that his harp would be heard one Sunday in the church, but he himself would not be there. According to the story, just as he had prophesised, the harp was heard to play . . . but the harpist himself was never seen again! His music, however, could still be heard from time to time.

A similar tale relates to the cave spring at Ffynnon Ddu (SN 843157) in the Swansea valley. Back in the mists of time an itinerant animal castrator was supposed to have disappeared into a cave hereabouts. As he disappeared from sight, he was heard blowing a horn that he always carried. The tale was still recited by some local folk even early in the twentieth century but, despite the presumed existence of a cave somewhere beneath the mountain, no accessible passage was known. The only route into the hillside appeared to be via an impassable flooded tunnel from which water emerged. Then, in 1946, cavers excavated a hole a short distance from the spring and gained access to what is today one of Britain's longest cave networks. A short time later the explorers discovered a human skeleton in a small chamber. The mystery has never been satisfactorily explained.

A few underground sites possess romantic associations. Perhaps the best known of these is the sea cave sometimes known as Reynard's Cave (SS 947677), at Tresilian Bay, near St Donat's. Tradition maintains that this is the cave of Dwynwen, the Celtic equivalent of the goddess Venus. Here, at low tide, young people would come with thoughts of marriage:

> Where nymphs and swains resort to see
> Fair Dwynwen's bow of destiny;
> And, by athletic feat to know
> Their near or distant marriage date,
> Their path prescribed by line below
> Their course inviolate.

Here, a short distance into the cave, a young man or girl would attempt to throw a stone over the top of a natural rock bridge situated beneath the roof of the tunnel. It was said that should the thrower succeed at the very first attempt, he or she would be married within the year. If more than one stone was thrown over the arch the person would be married more than once.

Apart from the folklore and legend associated with caves, it is interesting to note that miners also held many superstitions. For example, many believed that whistling underground would invoke evil spirits, whilst others claimed knowledge of the 'knockers' – 'y cnocwyr' – often described as 'little withered, dried-up creatures'. These dwarf or elf-like beings were said to resemble small children with large ugly heads, faces like old men, and ungainly limbs. They, too, were thought to work in the mines and the term 'knockers' came from the characteristic tapping noises that they made with their hammers. This belief was common, particularly in lead-mining districts throughout the British Isles. Generally, the 'knockers' were considered friendly folk, and the miners thought they did especially meritorious service by leading them to valuable mineral veins, as the tapping was usally heard in 'rich' ground. But they could also be vindictive, especially if a miner shouted at them or neglected to follow the custom of leaving a part of his dinner on the ground for their enjoyment!

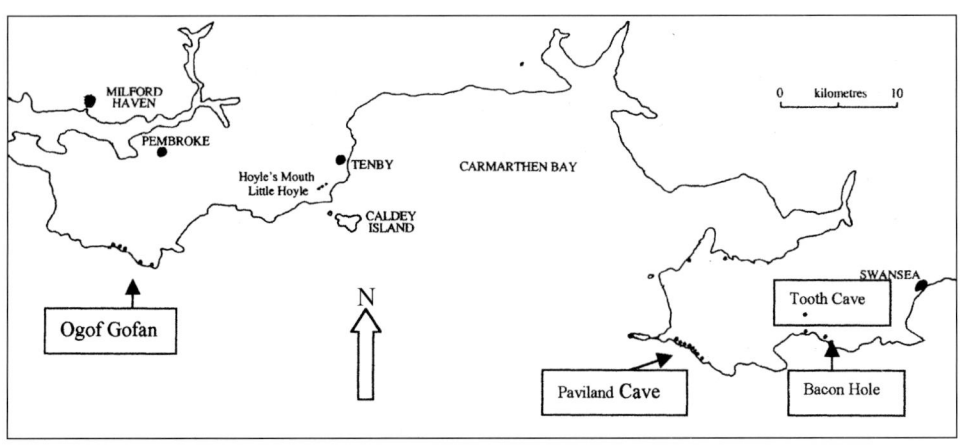

Archaeological cave sites in south Pembrokeshire and Gower.

A number of caves in Wales have also yielded valuable archaeological information. Excavations in places such as Paviland Cave (SS 437859) on the Gower coast have revealed a wealth of material dating back to the early Palaeolithic period – the Stone Age – indicative of settlement in the area possibly as early as 26,000 years ago. Indeed, this particular site is one of the most important caves in the British Isles with regard to the Stone Age artefacts uncovered. Sites in south Pembrokeshire, such as Hoyle's Mouth cave (SN 112003) near Tenby, are also significant in this respect. Similarly, a number of cave sites in north-east Wales have greatly aided our understanding of settlement in the region. Pontnewydd (SJ 015710) and Cefn caves (SJ 021705), a few miles north-west of Denbigh, have been found to contain the oldest human bones so far discovered in Wales. Studies here have led to the conclusion that man began his occupation of this area as early as 250,000 to 230,000 years ago. In addition, the bones of many animals have been discovered, including warmth-loving, straight-tusked elephant, soft-nosed rhinoceros, and hippopotamus. With the onset of glaciation these animals were forced to retreat south, the first two

becoming extinct, while the hippopotamus survives only in Africa. It is important to recall that during the glacial episodes Britain was physically linked, via a land bridge, with the continent of Europe. With much of the Earth's water locked up in the form of large ice-caps, sea-level around our shores may have been 100 metres or more lower than the present-day.

The impressive headland of the Great Orme, at Llandudno, has also yielded a wealth of archaeological material. Apart from the caves being used as places for shelter, it is clear that man, during the

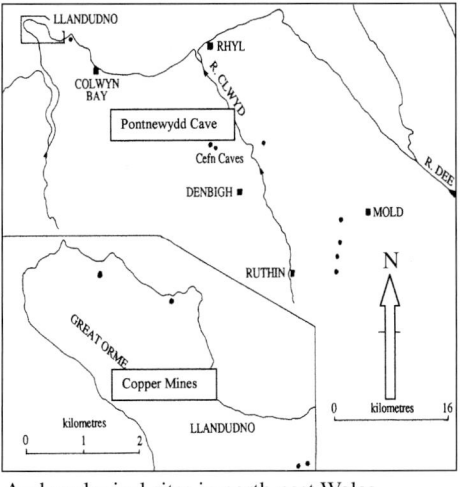

Archaeological sites in north-east Wales.

Paviland Cave, Gower.

Bronze Age, commenced mining the copper ore in the limestone. Substantial man-made tunnels and caverns have been revealed here in recent times and found to contain a wealth of artefacts dating back over 3,000 years. The Great Orme Copper Mine (SH 769831) has today been developed as a show-mine complex and here the visitor will be amazed at the sheer extent of this ancient but extremely important industry.

The Bone Cave (Ogof yr Esgyrn) in the upper Swansea valley has also been developed as an interpretive centre and is part of the Dan yr Ogof show-cave complex. Studies conducted earlier last century show clear evidence of this cave being used as a burial site. The remains of some 40 people were exhumed here, dating from perhaps 3,000 years ago until the late Roman period (400 AD). Other discoveries made during the investigations included a gold bead, a bronze 'razor' and the blade of a bronze dirk or short sword. This last item, some 343 mm (13.5 inches) long, is presumed to date from between 1050 BC and 850 BC. Nine Roman coins – all providing valuable dating material for the occupation – were also recovered together with pottery, bone pins and bronze awls.

Across Wales as a whole many other caves and subterranean shelters have yet to be thoroughly investigated. Indeed, as our knowledge of archaeology develops and as investigative techniques improve, it is abundantly clear that our interpretation of certain sites and events may need revision. The archaeological study of the caves and mines of Wales is far from complete. In the fullness of time exciting discoveries are assured.

LIMESTONE

With the exception of sea caves and other small rock shelters, often referred to locally as a 'cave', true cave systems are found predominantly in limestone. Carboniferous Limestone occurs in two main areas in Wales. A major belt surrounds the saucer-shaped South Wales coalfield, while a smaller outcrop is found in north-east Wales. Whilst sea caves are formed by the erosive and battering action of waves, caves inland are solutional in origin; that is, water slowly dissolves the rock to form the caves. There are literally hundreds if not thousands of such caves in Wales, many of which are highly-acclaimed world-wide not only for their length but also with regard to the marvels they contain.

Caves, such as Dan yr Ogof in the upper Swansea valley, depend on three things for their existence: soluble rock, a flow of water, and time. The solubility of limestone is increased due to the fact that as rainwater passes through the atmosphere it absorbs carbon dioxide to become more aggressive in the form of a weak carbonic acid. Limestone itself is naturally fractured and water, under the influence of gravity, seeps into cracks and fissures (bedding planes and joints). As water gains access to the heart of the limestone, it begins its dual action of destruction and construction. At a later stage, when one particular crack or fissure reaches a certain critical size, it will capture the water from the surrounding rock. With increased flow the process of dissolving the limestone accelerates and slowly, ever so slowly, a seeping, waterlogged fissure will be transformed into a cave.

At the very earliest or phreatic stage of cave development the underground passage will be completely flooded. Later, when water levels drop – which happens, for example, as major rivers carve ever deeper into their valley floors, or as glaciers gouge and over-deepen their channels – some passageways will be completely transformed. Instead of being totally flooded, some tunnels will be partially drained and occupied by a free-flowing stream which gradually cuts into the cave floor. Other old waterways may become completely abandoned and are thereafter referred to as fossil passages.

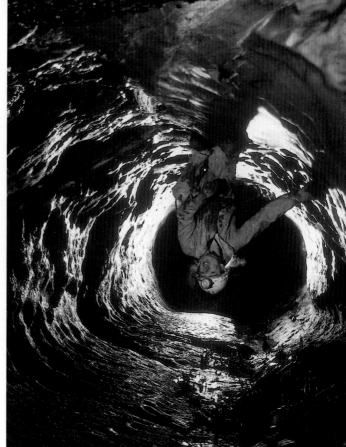

Phreatic tube, Tooth Cave, Green Cwm, Gower.

Ogof Draenen, Pwll Du, near Blaenavon.

Straw stalactites in Ogof Capel, Clydach gorge.

Passages that were once completely full of water have a distinctive round or elliptical cross-section. In the later or vadose stage of development, when a stream runs along the cave floor, the cave frequently exhibits trench-like features associated with down-cutting. Put very simply, first-stage passages are characterised by wonderful tubular shapes, while second-stage developments frequently form tall narrow fissures or canyons. Many passages will have a combination of these features, and in cross-section present a typical 'key-hole' profile.

Other features associated with the erosional development of caves include deep shafts or potholes and large chambers or caverns. Potholes are found at places where water has, at some stage, found an easy route vertically through the rock layers; caverns, on the other hand, may develop where two major fissures intersect and their floors are frequently littered with boulders which have collapsed from the roof above.

While on the one hand Mother Nature seeks to carve out and modify the passageways through the limestone, so too does she seek to decorate this world of darkness. Here and there we find sights of rare, exquisite beauty. These decorations or cave formations are, like the caves themselves, a product of water. As the water percolates slowly through the fissures in the rock it carries with it small quantities of dissolved limestone. Once the seeping water finds its way into an air space within a cave passage it will release some of the carbon dioxide gas dissolved in it. This in turn results in some of the dissolved rock being precipitated in the form of a white crystalline substance known as calcite. A small drop of water emerging on the roof of a cave passage will deposit a minute quantity of calcite before it falls to the floor. Day after day, over a period of hundreds or even thousands of years, the process continues, resulting in the formation of a pure white, delicate, straw stalactite. Occasionally the hollow space at the centre of the straw column will block and the seeping liquid will ooze out just above the constriction. Many years later the stalactite will appear like some pendulous 'carrot-shaped' formation.

When the water droplet falls to the cave floor – provided, of course, there is no stream present to wash it away – yet more calcite is laid down. This results in the formation of a stumpy, solid mass which grows slowly upward to form a stalagmite. When a stalactite and stalagmite meet, the outcome is a pillar or column, such as that found at the end of Flabbergasm Chasm in Dan yr Ogof. Sometimes the calcite-laden flow will produce different but equally spectacular formations: convoluted, ribbed and banded curtains, for example, such as that seen in the upper series in Ogof Ffynnon Ddu 2 (the cave in the hillside opposite Dan yr Ogof). Occasionally, the calcite flow will quite literally paint the dark walls with a pristine porcelain gloss and then perhaps meander away across the flat cave floor. Such formations resemble frozen rivers, especially when individual crystals sparkle in the beam of a caver's caplamp. Within such a setting, curious little dams and intricate networks of minute ponds, the sides of which are lined with jagged crystals, can also be found. To the caver these are known as gour pools. The strangest formations are helictites, crystal structures which jut from the wall or floor of caves, or even the side of stalactites. Typically, these will defy gravity by twisting, turning and growing upwards! Quite how, or why, these exquisite little features occupy the sites they do is still poorly understood.

Dripstone formations vary in terms of size, colour and orientation; what is paramount is that they, like all formations,

Helictites, Dan yr Ogof,
Swansea valley.

Stalactites and stalagmites,
Ogof Darren Cilau, Llangattock

should remain as they were first discovered. A fragile crystal structure, which may have taken thousands of years to form, can be destroyed in the blink of an eye, a priceless wonder lost for all time.

Caves are in a very real sense the repositories of untold knowledge; time brings many changes and this mysterious world beneath our feet can tell us much about the planet upon which we live.

The Limestone and Caves of South Wales

Otter Hole, Chepstow.

The limestone scenery of South Wales is often spectacular, nowhere more so than underground. The limestone extends beneath Blorenge, overlooking Abergavenny, and thereafter in a continuous narrow band trending west, above Llangattock, along the southern rim of the Brecon Beacons, Fforest Fawr and the Black Mountain, eventually terminating at the dramatic, sheer cliffs along the coast of south Pembrokeshire. Another comparable and significant area of limestone extends from Caldicot to Chepstow and into the Forest of Dean. Particulary imposing are the cliffs along the meandering course of the river Wye, at places such as Symmons Yat and Windcliff.

Otter Hole, Chepstow (ST 526961)
With its entrance passage situated in the tidal reaches of the river Wye, Otter Hole is unique in British caving circles. The cave was discovered in the early 1970s and given its location, entry (and exit!) is only possible at low tide. This means that visiting parties must plan and execute their day's caving meticulously. Negotiating the first 600 metres is somewhat akin to an obstacle course, which involves traversing thick, glutinous mud and slurry. Thereafter the caver ascends to a higher level of passageways, a silent realm, completely free of water. Here 80 or 90 metres directly below Chepstow Racecourse the cave is completely transformed. Dripstone deposits suddenly loom and seemingly multiply out of the darkness. The wonders defy description. Otter Hole is arguably the most spectacular cave in the British Isles.

OGOF DRAENEN (SO 246118)

To the south of the Clydach gorge – between the towns of Abergavenny, Brynmawr and Pontypool – lies one of the best kept secrets of the Welsh underworld. Caving enthusiasts had long suspected that a fairly extensive cave might lie beneath Gilwern Hill and Blorenge but, try as they might, all attempts to gain entry to anything worthwhile seemed doomed to failure. Then, in 1994, a dedicated team of Cardiff-based cavers excavated their way down through a boulder-filled shaft and broke into the cavern of their dreams. To say that the discoveries exceeded their wildest imagination is an understatement. Visit after visit produced kilometre after kilometre of hitherto unexplored passages, and within a month the cave had topped 15 km in length. By the year 2000 the figure had increased to over 68 km and there is little doubt that this cave possesses many more secrets yet to be uncovered. In terms

of length and complexity the system has few rivals; indeed, it seems destined to become the longest cave system in the British Isles. The band of limestone in which Ogof Draenen is located is notable in that it trends south-east from the Clydach gorge all the way to Pontypool, some 11 km distant. It would appear that the area is literally honeycombed with cave passages. To postulate an overall length for this system is impossible but one day it may even be linked to the long-established Llangattock system lying to the west, on the other side of the river Clydach.

The Time Machine,
Ogof Darren Cilau.

The entrance passage of Ogof
Darren Cilau, Llangattock.

THE LLANGATTOCK CAVES

High on the hillside above Crickhowell, overshadowing the Usk valley, lies another of the longest cave networks in the British Isles. The first major discoveries in this area date from 1957 but since that time a very extensive cave system has been mapped, and may be followed all the way to the Clydach gorge, between Bryn-mawr and Gilwern. The charting of these caves has been an exciting and epic saga. There are in essence three major caves: Ogof Agen Allwedd (SO 187159) (34 km), Ogof Darren Cilau (SO 205153) (27 km) and Ogof Craig a Ffynnon (SO 220128) (9 km), together with a host of smaller caves. While these are presently unconnected it is known that they are part of one giant complex which was formed many millions of years ago. Together the combined length of the network is well in excess of 70 km but when, in the fullness of time, exploration continues into presently uncharted terrain it is likely that the length will exceed 100 km, possibly even 150 km. This mountain boasts the largest passages in the British Isles, passages attaining 30 metres (100 feet) in width and height. The caves also contain amazingly intricate crystal structures which have proven unique in the British Isles. Furthermore, some of the passages are also extremely important winter bat roosts, where colonies of some of the rarest bats in the British Isles, such as the Lesser Horseshoe, hibernate during the long winter months. As a result of all these special features the entire mountain has been designated a Site of Special Scientific Interest. Under the auspices of the Countryside Council for Wales a special team of experts has been established to advise on the future conservation of this unique cave system.

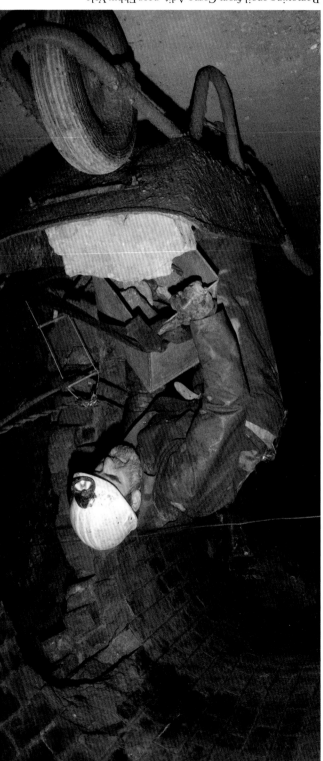

Removing spoil from Carno Adit, near Ebbw Vale.

CARNO ADIT (SO 164127)

Carno Adit is a man-made tunnel excavated into the hillside above Ebbw Vale with the intention of tapping the water reserves some three miles distant, on the other side of Mynydd Llangynidr. Dug between 1908 and 1912, the tunnellers encountered a number of natural cave openings purely by chance. Rather than transport the drams of spoil all the way out to the surface at Rassa, some of the deeper voids and shafts provided ideal sites for the dumping of waste rock. Eventually, severe geological difficulties were encountered and work ceased approximately half way to their goal. For many years the tunnel was forgotten. Then, in the late 1980s, cavers gained access to the site and turned their attention to the points used by the miners for back-filling with tunnel waste. There was very good reason to believe that such substantial fissures and shafts were part and parcel of a major cave system, a theory given all the more credence by the strong airflow present at the points of infill. After years of painstaking endeavour, which involved clearing at least one spacious shaft to a depth of 16 metres, the cavers gained access to an intricate labyrinth of passages presently totalling over nine kilometres. At the extremities of this dark and gloomy network, unexplored passages or 'leads' suggest the presence of a large intricate system of huge exploratory potential. There is a very strong flow of water at the furthest, flooded extremity of the system and hydrological study has shown that this eventually reappears at Ffynnon Gisfaen water pumping station some four kilometres distant, at the head of the Clydach gorge. A considerable amount of exploration still remains to be undertaken at this cave.

CHARTIST'S CAVE (SO 128152)

Chartist's Cave, Mynydd Llangynidr.

Although the entrance is deceptively large and accessible, finding this particular cave is not an easy task. Situated a mile from the nearest road, on the bleak and windswept Llangynidr moors, this was said to be the site where, in the dark years of the late 1830s, dissident leaders of the Chartist movement met in secret to formulate their schemes to overthrow the government of the day. The move towards full-scale revolution culminated in a tragic and ill-fated march to seize Newport in November 1839. In 1970, cavers attempting to explore the inner depths of the cavern uncovered human remains which have been subsequently dated by pathologist, Dr Bernard Knight, and ascribed to the late 1830s. These dismembered bones were clearly of murder victims, severed by what was described as a 'hand axe or butcher's cleaver'. Who these people may have been is open to conjecture but they certainly came to a grisly end!

North of Tredegar and west of the old quarry village of Trefil lies a vast expanse of moorland underlain by limestone. Several caves are known in the area, the longest of which being Ogof Tarddiad Rhymni (SO 085141) in the now abandoned Ystrad Quarries. Neither Ogof Tarddiad Rhymni nor Ogof ap Robert (SO 099134) are particularly easy to find but both contain fine passages, large chambers

Ogof ap Robert, near Trefil.

The Gunbarrel. Ogof y Ci,
near Merthyr Tydfil.

and good draughts – the sure sign of many more caves waiting to be found. Both are well over one kilometre in length.

OGOF Y CI (SO 040104)

Ogof y Ci, situated in the Nant y Glais valley, north of Merthyr Tydfil, is a fairly popular cave amongst novice groups. The complex as a whole is over 500 metres in length and presents little in the way of technical difficulty. The section illustrated is affectionately known as the Gunbarrel, but much of the rest of the system consists of easy walking terrain.

SCHWYLL WATER PUMPING STATION
(SS 88771)

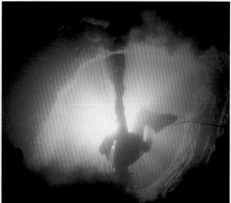

Flooded Passage, Schwyll Pumping Station, Ewenny.

At Ewenny, on the outskirts of Bridgend, lies one of the largest freshwater springs in Britain. For hundreds of years it has supplied local residents and, in more recent times, much of the Vale of Glamorgan with pure, unfailing water. In the late 1920s a major pumping station was established and this subsequently supplied over 5 million gallons a day. But the source of the water was something of a mystery as there was no accessible 'dry' cave and no clear geological evidence as to its origin. In 1998, however, the author was allowed access and, following a series of solo cave-diving operations, an intricate network of flooded passages trending in an east-south-easterly direction was charted. These presently amount to over one kilometre in length.

PORTH YR OGOF (SN 928124)
Porth yr Ogof is one of the most impressive caves in Britain. It lies near the small village of Ystradfellte, on the southern boundary of the Brecon Beacons National Park. The cave boasts the largest entrance in Wales, indeed one of the largest in the British Isles. It is in every respect a

special place: the setting, the atmosphere, the insight it provides to the wonders of the natural world beneath our feet, renders it an ideal venue for introductory caving activity.

The cave has been a well-known spectacle for many hundreds of years and early descriptions of the site provide interesting reading. Michael Faraday, the acclaimed nineteenth-century scientist, provided a particularly accurate account of the cave following his visit in 1819. In the company of a local guide, hired in Pontneddfechan, Faraday walked up the Mellte valley to Porth yr Ogof:

We entered with the stream upon its pebbled and bouldered bank and groped our way in diminishing daylight until the roar of surrounding streams made us fearful of advance and the guide then by throwing stones before made us conscious of the deep pool of water

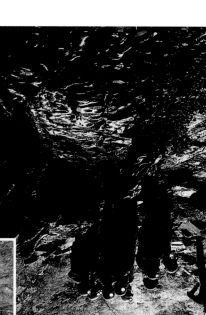

The main entrance to
Porth yr Ogof, Ystradfellte.

After the trip, Porth yr Ogof, Ystradfellte.

which terminated our way. Returning from this retired place where the eye could scarcely be used, but where the ear was stunned by sounds, we lighted candles and then, stooping, creeping, stumbling, we proceeded through the hollows of the limestone into the bowels of the mountain. Stalactites covered our heads and embarrassed our feet but here and there, immense beds of sand offered steady footing and chambers formed by nature gave room for free motion. I crossed the river with the guide to view some other parts of the cavern and proceeded a great way

inwards. Here and there cavities ascended upwards many, many feet and let in daylight through chinks in the mountain and its sudden affusion every now and then over the objects below was very delightful in a ramble in what might be called darkness, for our candles were lost in the black space about us.

Today well over 30,000 people a year – mainly young people staying at residential outdoor education centres in the locality – visit Porth yr Ogof to savour the unique underground experience.

THE NEATH VALLEY

Accessed via a long, narrow country lane, a series of caves, frequented by novices and more experienced cavers alike, lies at the headwaters of the Nedd Fechan. Novices will delight in Bridge Cave (SN 912140), White Lady Cave (SN 911137) and Town Drain (SN 911136), none of which will occupy them for more than an hour or two. But the real gem here is a cave called Little Neath River Cave (SN 912142), a classic in Wales and one of the finest sporting caves in the world. Its entrance lies in the very bed of Afon Nedd Fechan and given the fact that it is hardly bigger than the opening to a badger set it is clearly a system to be avoided in all but drought conditions. However, in drier summer weather this is one of the most splendid underground excursions that any caver will ever undertake. After worming along a rocky tunnel with water flowing up and over his or her back, it comes as something of a welcome relief when, after a crawl of some 45 metres, the caver suddenly emerges and is able to tread comfortably along glorious, clean, water-worn tunnel, with lots of calcite formations and huge mist-filled caverns.

The entrance crawl, Little Neath River Cave.

OGOF FFYNNON DDU (SN 848153)

For many years Ogof Ffynnon Ddu was the longest and deepest cave system in the British Isles. This wonderful cave lies under the eastern flank of the upper Swansea valley, a short way up-valley of the village of Aber-craf. It has three entrances some distance apart and the underground journey between any of these is one for the more experienced caver only. The sheer beauty and complexity of the cave is hard to comprehend and well over 50 km of passages have been charted, extending over a vertical range of some

Ogof Ffynnon Ddu, Swansea valley.

Calcite curtain, Ogof Ffynnon Ddu, Swansea valley.

300 metres. Passages criss-cross one above the other forming one of the most intricate labyrinths imaginable. The various levels of cave development attest to the vast age of the system, while the most recent is that where the active stream flows today. This passage is truly superb in every respect. The tunnel is spectacularly sculpted and atmospheric; the clean, washed walls glisten in the headlight, there are deep water-worn swirl holes in the floor and, in places, the caver experiences the caving equivalent of a giant cresta run. It takes several hours to make a subterranean traverse between any of the entrances but for all cavers, a visit to Ogof Ffynnon Ddu is something akin to a pilgrimage.

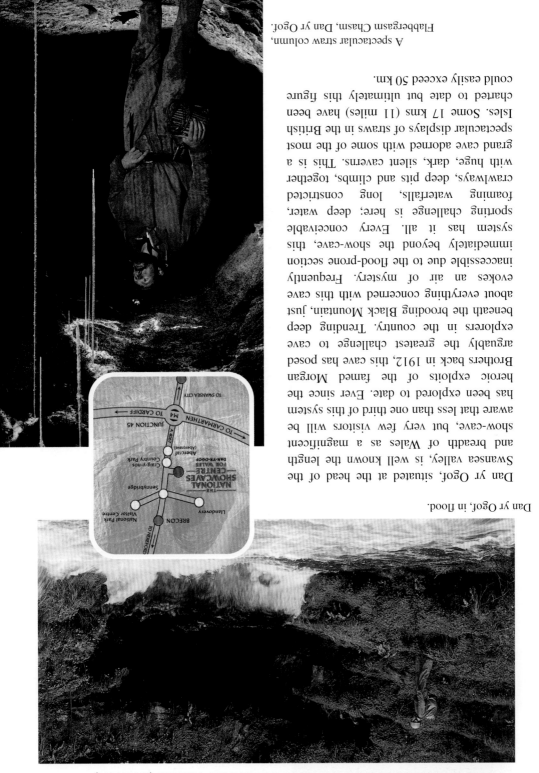

DAN YR OGOF:
THE NATIONAL SHOWCAVES CENTRE FOR WALES (SN 838160)

Dan yr Ogof, in flood.

Dan yr Ogof, situated at the head of the Swansea valley, is well known the length and breadth of Wales as a magnificent show-cave, but very few visitors will be aware that less than one third of this system has been explored to date. Ever since the heroic exploits of the famed Morgan Brothers back in 1912, this cave has posed arguably the greatest challenge to cave explorers in the country. Trending deep beneath the brooding Black Mountain, just about everything concerned with this cave evokes an air of mystery. Frequently inaccessible due to the flood-prone section immediately beyond the show-cave, this system has it all. Every conceivable sporting challenge is here; deep water, foaming waterfalls, long constricted crawlways, deep pits and climbs, together with huge, dark, silent caverns. This is a grand cave adorned with some of the most spectacular displays of straws in the British Isles. Some 17 kms (11 miles) have been charted to date but ultimately this figure could easily exceed 50 km.

A spectacular straw column,
Flabbergasm Chasm, Dan yr Ogof.

Pwll Dwfn pothole, near Dan yr Ogof.

PWLL DWFN (SN 834165)

Situated high on the Black Mountain above Dan yr Ogof, Pwll Dwfn is Wales' deepest pothole. The entrance is an inconspicuous, small opening, set in a shallow dry valley, but below ground a series of five separate shafts provide a spectacular descent of 93 metres. Given the fact that the pothole lies only 500 metres from Dan yr Ogof it is tempting to speculate that some form of connection will eventually be established between the two caves.

LLYGAD LLWCHWR (SN 669178)

This discreet spring of the River Loughor (Afon Llwchwr), close to Carreg Cennen castle, is the site of one of the first recorded cave explorations in Wales. It was here in the early 1840s that a certain Thomas Jenkins of Llandeilo ventured underground in the company of a group of equally adventurous companions in an attempt to discover some of the mysteries of the Welsh underworld. Narrow passageways restrict the entrance area but the inner recesses are effectively closed to all by deep, flooded sections. Jenkins used a fisherman's coracle to ply the dark waters and, to his credit, explored most of the cave. Today, cavers may occasionally utilise an inflatable dinghy.

Llygad Llwchwr, near Carreg Cennen castle.

THE CAVES OF GOWER

The Gower peninsula is officially designated an Area of Outstanding Natural Beauty, attributable in large measure to the lofty limestone cliffs that line its southern edge. While the casual visitor may have viewed the fine arch at Three Cliffs and perhaps the 'smugglers' cave', known as Culver Hole (SS 406930), at Port Eynon, few will be aware of other longer caves both along the coast itself and inland. Some of the 'sea caves' provided shelter for the very earliest inhabitants in the region. In fact, archaeological study of sites such as Paviland Cave (SS 437859) and Bacon Hole (SS 561868) has shed much light on the pattern of settlement in prehistoric times. Detailed studies of these caves began as early as the 1820s when the Reverend William Buckland dug up a human skeleton that had lain on the floor of Paviland Cave. As it was stained with natural red ochre it became known as 'The Red Lady of Paviland'. Only much later in the twentieth century was it discovered that the remains were actually those of a male dating back about 26,000 years. Significantly, perhaps, the skeleton was found next to a mammoth's skull, complete with tusks. It is also interesting to reflect that by about 20,000 years ago the edge of the nearest glacier ice may have been just an hour's walk to the north. At that time the area was, in a real sense, at the very edge of the then known world. Culver Hole is something of a regional curiosity. Romantic folklore often connects such caves with the activities of smugglers but in this case very little is known concerning the walled-off cleft in the rocks. According to legend, a local prince, Eynon, after defeat in battle, retired to the site

Culver Hole, Gower.

and erected something akin to a pirates' castle. It was certainly a stronghold but its true significance remains a mystery.

Caves situated further inland were also occupied by early man and Tooth Cave (SS 532911) in the upper reaches of the peaceful, wooded valley behind Parkmill has yielded a wealth of human artefacts dating back to the Bronze Age. Excavations here unearthed eight skeletons suggesting that the cave was used as a burial site.

Fine curtain formations, Llethryd Swallet, Gower.

Ogof Gofan, near Bosherston.

THE CAVES OF PEMBROKESHIRE

The dramatic sea cliffs fringing the southern coast of Pembrokeshire are the domain of leading British rock climbers, who routinely undertake some breathtaking ascents on what may appear to be utterly impossible rock faces. However, west of Tenby, near the hamlet of Bosherston, lie rarely visited caves of some considerable beauty. Hanging from a single rope some 45 metres above the crashing waves renders this odyssey distinctly challenging even for the most experienced caver, but the venture is certainly well worthwhile once the cave is finally accessed. To visit Ogof Gofan (SR 959929) and view the inner reaches of the cavern is a great privilege.

The Limestone and Caves of North Wales

Limestone is less widespread in North Wales than in the south, the main outcrop trending in a relatively narrow band from Llangollen almost directly north to the sea. While limestone outcrops may be visually impressive in the Llangollen area, the geology is rather more intriguing further north. Geologically, this is a very complex area with significant concentrations of minerals occurring within the limestone. The natural underground systems discovered to date are rather limited in size and extent, in comparison to their counterparts in South Wales, but the man-made tunnels and mines associated with them certainly are not. Six kilometres west of Mold, for example, the River Alyn, a tributary of the Dee, reaches the limestone. In a similar situation to that prevailing in the vicinity of the headwaters of the River Neath in South Wales, the river discreetly disappears via various cracks and fissures into underlying cavities and caves, until eventually its course is completely dry. However, despite clear evidence as to the existence of caves, significant discoveries were to elude local cave explorers for many years. The quest was intensified following the study of mining records. These clearly showed that the water disappearing in the bed of the Alyn found its way into lead workings deep underground and that the miners themselves had made numerous attempts to prevent the surface water from interfering with their work. Their efforts, however, did not meet with a high degree of success. Such was the extent of the problem, and the potential rewards that stood to be gained, that the final solution to free the mines of water involved the constuction of an elaborate and very costly mine drainage scheme, achieved by driving level tunnels into the base of the hills from the coast to the north. The most effective of these was the Milwr Tunnel.

The Milwr Tunnel (SJ 222754)

The Milwr Tunnel, constructed between 1897 and 1957, was driven from just above sea level at Bagillt for a distance of 16 km (10 miles). This 'drain' had a profound effect on a number of natural caves in the area, by draining passageways which, in their original state, would probably have been completely flooded. As the tunnel was driven forward it intersected several flooded natural cavities, sometimes with dramatic results. In 1917, for example, near the village of Windmill, such a cavern was breached and the water flooding out was sufficient to sweep fully-loaded waggons some distance down the tunnel. Eleven hours later, St Winefride's Well at Holywell, some 4 km (2.5 miles) away and about 100 metres above sea level, ran dry. The Milwr Tunnel still performs the same function today, despite the fact that lead mining has long since ceased in the area.

One of the most impressive natural caverns in the system is Powell's Lode, deep beneath the village of Rhosesmor. This spectacular chamber was found by miners in 1931 and measures 40 metres high by 70 metres long. To one side lies a lake of very deep, clear blue water which discharges 5,000 gallons of water a minute (1,400 cubic metres a second) directly into the main tunnel. Given the substantial outflow, the miners were unable to drain the lake which is known to be over 60 metres deep. As yet, the origin of the enormous descending passageway is a complete mystery.

It was not until 1973 that a group of dedicated explorers finally discovered a major cave near the hamlet of Cilcain. To date, Ogof Hesp Alyn (SJ 188653) has been mapped for approximately two kilometres and descends to a depth of 79 metres (260 feet) below river level. The place is most unusual inasmuch as the cave

Powell's Lode, Rhosesmor.

lies below the water-table. This, combined with the almost overpowering quietness, the general gloom, the fact that everything still fills up with water in time of flood, gives the cave a distinctly menacing flavour all of its own. In addition, mud coats the walls, floor and indeed the roof: a cave to be treated with the utmost respect by visiting cavers!

Water from Ogof Hesp Alyn enters the Milwr Tunnel about 2 km south of the old Olwyn Goch lead mine, situated at Hendre. Today, this is one of the cavers' principal access points to a vast underground labyrinth that includes Powell's Lode. Some 5 million gallons a day pour into the Milwr Tunnel from Ogof Hesp Alyn and this, combined with the water rising from the unexplored cave system entering at Powell's Lode, 1.5 km north of Olwyn Goch Shaft, gives rise to a substantial

waterway. However, although these two inflows are the largest contributors of water to the tunnel, by the time the water surfaces at Bagillt the volume has doubled again to 23 million gallons a day to form an impressive river!

Apart from the sections of 'natural' passages rendered accessible by the shaft at Olwyn Goch, there is one other amazing sight that no cave or mine enthusiast would want to miss – the vast underground limestone workings. Within just a short distance of the 120 metre deep shaft lie enormous limestone quarries and scattered about the complex are all manner of mining hardware, including heavy rock drills, trams, locomotives and specialised mechanical rock shovels.

Limestone workings, Olwyn Goch mine, Hendre.

COAL

The use of coal as a fuel, particularly where seams outcropped at the surface, has a long history. Near Saundersfoot, in Pembrokeshire, for example, coal was worked in 1324. However, despite seemingly obvious advantages when compared to wood, coal was not a popular fuel. It contains impurities which gave rise to noxious fumes and so, given the poor ventilation of early houses, the use of wood and its by-product, charcoal, was preferred. The same problems hampered many early attempts to use coal as an industrial fuel.

Geologically, coal is found in two main areas of Wales: so-called Coal Measures, containing coal seams, occupy a narrow belt running parallel with the Welsh border in north-east Wales, and extend across much of South Wales. Mining began in earnest where coal was easily accessible, at places such as Blaenavon (Monmouthshire), now designated a World Heritage Site; Llandybïe (Carmarthenshire); Cefn Onn, near

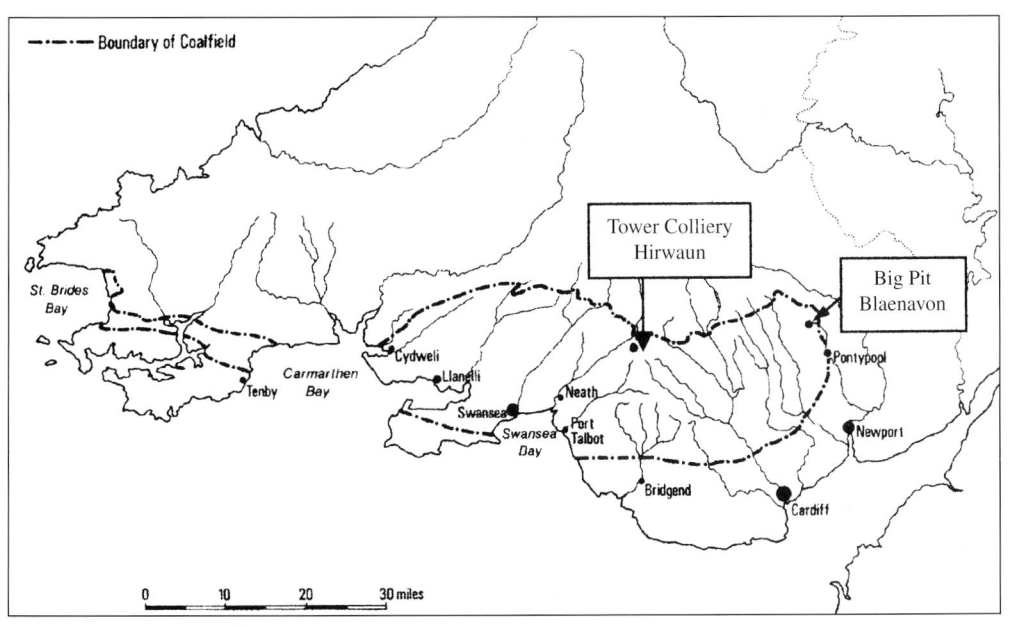

The South Wales Coalfield.

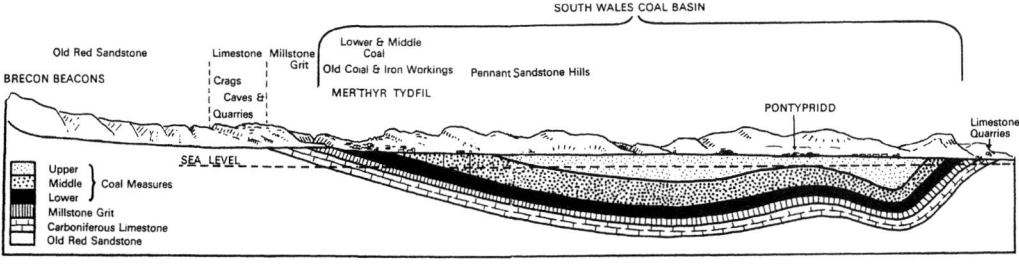

Cross-section of South Wales Coalfield.

39

Caerphilly; Pyle and Margam; Clyne, near Swansea; Resolven in the Vale of Neath; Llanelli; Johnston, Begelly and Roch in Pembrokeshire; and Ewloe in north-east Wales. In general, the early coal workings at such localities involved the digging of very shallow pits (bell pits) or horizontally driven tunnels, known as levels or drifts. By the 1580s coal was being exported from Swansea and Neath and, during the seventeenth century, coal came into general use for smelting copper and lead, although attempts at smelting iron ore with coal were still far from satisfactory. However, given the rapidly rising demand for iron products and the decimation of native woodlands (the iron industry required approximately one acre of timber to produce three tons of metal) it was inevitable that experiments would be conducted in order to solve the problem of smelting ore with the aid of coal. The most significant breakthrough came in 1709 when the Quaker ironmaster Abraham Darby, based in Shropshire, successfully smelted iron ore with the aid of coke, a 'purified' form of coal. The stage was now set for the Industrial Revolution, which would hinge upon the use of coal, a resource in plentiful supply in both south and north-east Wales.

THE INDUSTRIAL REVOLUTION

The Industrial Revolution, kindled in the eighteenth century, resulted in the development of iron-smelting in centres strung along a belt of iron-bearing rocks found in the Coal Measures. In South Wales this narrow band extended from Blaenavon in the east to Hirwaun in the west, and at these places coal, or more precisely coke, came to replace charcoal for smelting. The revolution was sparked by demand, and the ease and availability of raw materials. These consisted of ironstone, coal, limestone (which assisted in the separation of the iron from the low-grade ore) and water power, which was necessary to provide the blast for the furnaces.

Large-scale industrial development in South Wales began in the late 1750s and by the mid 1790s there were a multitude of iron furnaces scattered along the northern perimeter of the South Wales coalfield. There were nine at Merthyr Tydfil alone, with others at Blaenavon, Nantyglo, Beaufort, Tredegar and Hirwaun. Coke was now in general use as a fuel and with an output of 34,000 tons of iron, the furnaces of South Wales were producing half the total for England and Wales.

Developments in the iron industry gave great stimulus to coal- and iron-mining alike. With the growth of steam power, especially the invention of steam-driven locomotion, the demand for these products was almost insatiable. As technology improved so mines slowly began to work the deeper seams of coal at the very heart of the coalfield. Apart from surface outcrops of the upper coal beds, the major coal reserves situated at depth were not worked until the mid to late nineteenth century. Indeed, it is significant to note that the first trainload of coal from the Rhondda did not enter Cardiff until 1855. With the development of 'deep' mining other problems arose, and foremost among these was the provision of adequate ventilation. No matter how large the space underground, the quality of the air was always a matter of concern. In coalmines accumulations of 'foul' air were common. The miner had to be constantly on the alert for 'blackdamp' – a mixture of carbon dioxide and nitrogen which in large quantities will suffocate candles and people alike. As the mines were driven deeper, 'firedamp' – a mixture of methane and air – was encountered. Firedamp was found to be highly inflammable, but apart from this the volume of coal-dust in the air also played a crucial role in the explosive equation.

It was in and around Merthyr Tydfil where the greatest concentration of ironworks and collieries was established. The scientist Michael Faraday visited the area in 1819 and his acute observation portrays a most dramatic scene:

> On approaching Merthyr, the great change upon the surface of the earth, indicated the extensive works beneath. Tramways ran in every direction, and every now and then a range of thirty or forty trams laden with coal, or ore, or limestone, illustrated the advantage of this mode of conveyance. On all sides, were piled up large mountains of slag, cinder and refuse; or sometimes of valuable materials or products, as coal, ironstone and iron. Men, black as gnomes, were moving in all directions, taking to and bringing from the furnaces, and works; and as we came into sight of these erections, flame upon flame appeared rising over the country and scorching the air.

Faraday was not to venture underground in this locality but an account published in the *Morning Chronicle* in 1850 is particularly noteworthy. Glyndyrys Pit was fairly typical of mines in the locality. It was a 'balance pit', whereby coal or iron (both were mined at this site) was brought to the surface by the simple but ingenious technique of using a form of counterbalance in the shaft, namely a container filled with water. The reporter descended the 140 metre deep (462 feet) shaft, and described the scene as follows:

> We directed our course in the first instance, to the iron mines, which are considerably below the coal. The

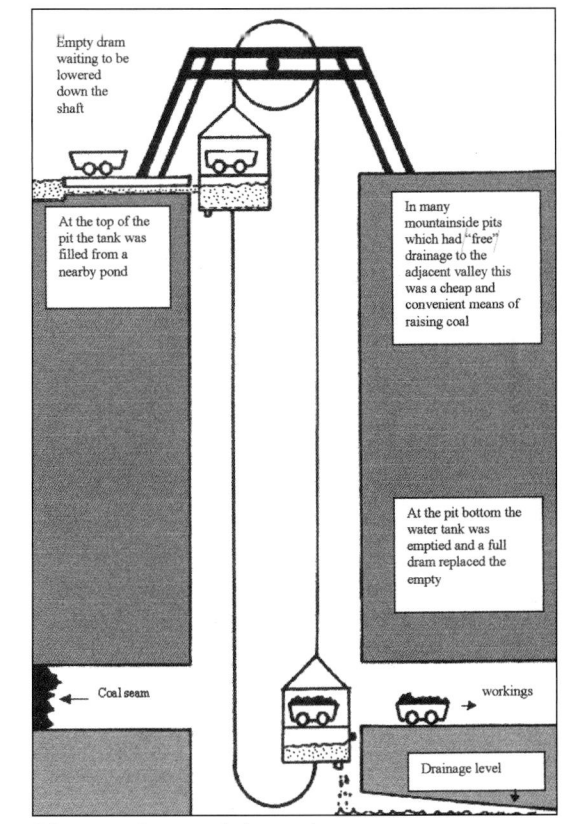

Diagram of a water balance pit.

closeness and heat of the pit were sensibly increased, and the difficulty of breathing was aggravated by thick clouds of sulphurous smoke from the blasting of the rock with gunpowder. Rumbling reverberations from successive 'blasts' in different directions mingled with the sharp short ring of the miners' 'picks', echoed through the roof with a strange effect upon the ear. Glimmering red through the smoke, we saw at length, and as it were at a vast distance, a few lights in motion; another hundred yards, and we had reached the stalls where the men were working.

The miner was boring the solid rock with a long iron chisel which he plied lustily with a heavy iron hammer, twisting it partly round to disengage the splintered materials between each stroke. He was a tall, wiry-made man, of some thirty years of age, clad in a flannel shirt open at the throat, and with the sleeves tucked above the elbows. Fustian trousers, shoes, and a handkerchief tightly bound about the head, completed his working dress. His face, though besmudged with the muddy water which dripped from the roof, was not black like that of colliers, in fact, is far more cleanly than that of the latter. The workings I visited were in what is called the 'blue vein', which is about four inches thick…

Leaving the iron mines, we directed our steps to the quarter where the coal is raised. The temperature of the workings is here considerably higher than in the iron mines, and the air, though moving, with the pressure of a gentle breeze, is charged with gas and minute particles of coal dust, equally unwholesome for respiration. Passing several doors for regulating the draught, we steadily ascended at a low gradient, kicking up clouds of small coal at each step we took, until we reached the stalls where the colliers were at work.

The roof was wet and dripping, my face, note book and clothes were by this time very freely bespattered so, I could scarcely make matters worse, I sat down on a block of coal. Behind me I heard a uniform and monotonously singing voice, like the humming of a gnat, only much louder, inquired what it was; he told me it was occasioned by the fire-damp, which made this sound in rushing through the fissures into the workings.

Old ironstone workings, Penydarren, Merthyr Tydfil.

42

I asked him to show me the place where it came in. Holding his candle to the floor of the coal, and sweeping away the rubbish with the other hand, it immediately fired, and continued burning over the crevice till he tramped it out. I wished to see a slight explosion, if it might be attempted without danger, and I was gratified. Cautioning us to stoop, the collier raised his candle with a rapid movement towards the roof, and as suddenly withdrew it, but without effect. The second time it fired, flashing like gunpowder, and moving with great velocity, and a whizzing noise a few yards forwards and backwards, and then it died out.

The inherent dangers presented by the underground environment were well known, yet sadly it took a great many tragedies before these problems were addressed and preventative measures implemented. Given the problem of firedamp, it was only a matter of time before places such as Merthyr Tydfil were to witness the tragedy and suffering of a major explosion. One such event occurred at the Lower Gethin Colliery, to the south of the town, on 19 February 1862. About 45 bodies were recovered that day, some of which were unidentifiable. On 20 December 1865 another explosion occurred at the Upper Gethin Colliery. On this occasion the fatalities amounted to six from severe burns, while 26 or 28 died from suffocation. According to the *Cardiff and Merthyr Guardian* reporter:

We have never seen such a spectacle – such a scene of horror. Those burnt were so charred about the face that any feature might have been broken off as one breaks a piece of charcoal. Their hair burnt away; hands clotted like jelly.

Similarly devastating explosions took place in other valleys:

1860 Risca Mine, near Newport, 145 killed
1867 Ferndale Colliery, Rhondda, 178 killed
1878 Abercarn Colliery, Monmouthshire, 268 killed
1894 Albion Colliery, Cilfynydd, Glamorgan, 290 killed

Tragic as these were, it was the small community of Senghennydd, near Caerphilly, that was to figure most prominently in the annals of British mining disasters. On 24 May 1901 some 81 men lost their lives at the Universal Colliery, a terrible harbinger of worse to follow. Twelve years later, on 14 October 1913, 439 men and boys died at the same colliery.

Predictably similar disasters took place in other coalmining areas. On 22 September 1934, for example, an explosion, followed, as was so often the case, by fire and suffocation, led to the deaths of 265 miners at Gresford Colliery, Denbighshire.

The price of coal was dear. A more comprehensive view of the death toll makes for an altogether grim picture. In the 47 years up to 1914, 13,285 men were killed in the mines of South Wales. Not all died as a result of explosions. The vast majority died from rock falls and crush injuries inherent in winning coal from the reluctant seams. Most of these men died in lonely and quickly forgotten circumstances. Furthermore, the above death toll refers only to mineworkers. It does not include the men who died in the process of sinking the pits.

An abandoned small mine overlooking the Sela opencast site, Glyn Neath.

A small disused level, Glyn Neath.

Output of coal in South Wales increased throughout the nineteenth century, reaching its peak in 1913 when some 56 million tonnes were produced. Over 217,000 people were directly employed in the industry in the mid 1920s but thereafter there was a steady, relentless decline. The growth of Cardiff was due in very large measure to the growing export trade in coal and in 1913 this city was the largest coal port in the world. At the peak of coal production, prior to the First World War, there were over 600 pits dotted across the coalfield. As with production figures, and the number of men employed, the number of collieries declined rapidly as the twentieth century progressed. There were 200 pits in 1950, producing approximately 20 million tonnes. In 1965 the number of collieries stood at 70. By 1980 output had declined to about 8 million tonnes and the following decade proved to be a dramatic period of pit closure. Only 11 mines remained in production in 1988 and 5 in 1990. By 1998 the sole remaining deep mine was Tower Colliery at Hirwaun. A combination of economic and political circumstances had brought the industry of old to its knees and today the majority of coal produced in the region is won by massive machines from immense open-cast pits, such as Cwm-gwrach above Blaen-gwrach in the Vale of Neath. In a global context it is significant to note that in the United States most of the coal is won with the aid of huge machines capable of mining over 10 metric tons per minute!

The Sela opencast coal site on the flanks of the Vale of Neath.

BIG PIT:
NATIONAL MINING MUSEUM OF WALES, BLAENAVON (SO 239088)

Blaenavon lies on the eastern edge of the South Wales coalfield and here the coal seams, which plunge below most of the valleys in the region, outcrop at the surface. Because the coal was relatively accessible early coal workings often took the form of near horizontal levels or drifts – tunnels which followed the slope of the coal seam back into the mountainside. Coalmining commenced here in the late eighteenth century, initially to supply the fuel for the iron furnaces. Later, the trade in coal became extremely important in its own right and miners were forced to tunnel further and ever deeper to obtain their rewards. An impression of the social and working conditions in the Blaenavon area may be gleaned from an official commission of enquiry which was published in 1842. Rees Jones, then aged 13, comments:

> I am a haulier, and drive a horse and tram in the mine-levels; I have been at work five years; I at first kept a door.

My father works in the level where I drive. I go out with the horse about six or seven o'clock in the morning, and work almost 12 hours every day. There are no regular times to stop; I often eat my bread and cheese on the tram going in and out; the horse has a 'nose-bag'. My father has five children; he has two girls besides me working – one 16, the other 12 years old; one is with my father, the other keeps an air-door.

Big Pit (created by deepening a shaft sunk about 1860) began producing coal in 1880 and during its working life miners extracted coal from nine separate seams. At the height of the mine's working life 1,300 men were employed, and produced over 250,000 tons of steam coal. Most of this supplied the railways in Britain, France, India and South America. With the slow decline in coal production in the twentieth century operations at Big Pit were scaled down and the colliery finally ceased as a producer in February 1980.

Big Pit, Blaenavon.

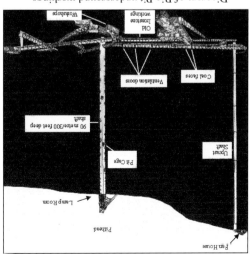

Diagram of Big Pit underground workings.

Subsequently, the mine reopened as a visitor centre in April 1983 and since that time approximately 100,000 visitors a year have passed through the complex. In November 2000 Blaenavon was designated a World Heritage Site in recognition of the area's historical importance on an international scale.

Big Pit or Pwll Mawr, now part and parcel of the National Museums and Galleries of Wales, is a place where the visitor may gain a first-hand impression of a typical Welsh coalmine. Preserved as a living and active reminder of our industrial past, it portrays the coalmining industry as it was during the nineteenth and twentieth centuries. No one can fail to be impressed by the experience: equipped with helmet, belt and miner's battery pack the visitor descends the 90 metre (300 feet) deep shaft and gains a wonderful insight to a once daily way of life for tens of thousands of miners, beneath the hills and valleys of South Wales.

TOWER COLLIERY, HIRWAUN (SN 927042)

Tower Colliery is the last remaining deep mine still working in Wales. The site lies below the steep, north-facing escarpment of Craig-y-llyn overlooking the upper Neath valley, whose headwaters drain the southern slopes of Forest Fawr within the Brecon Beacons National Park. To the south, just a few miles over the mountain, lies the famous Rhondda valley, epitomised in Richard Llewellyn's novel *How Green Was My Valley* (1939).

The shaft at Tower Colliery is about 162 metres (530 feet) deep, and was sunk between 1943 and 1946. Although the shaft lies at the organisational centre of mining operations – adjacent to the lamp room, the showers, and the offices – the coal itself is brought to the surface via a drift level some two kilometres distant. While the public are welcome to visit the site, underground tours are not permitted at the present time. Below

Tower Colliery, Hirwaun.

ground the workings are a constant hub of activity with a network of roadways and conveyors all focussing upon the working face several kilometres from the pit bottom. The passageways are surprisingly large and throughout most of the complex it is rare for tunnels to be less than three to four metres square. It also feels particularly warm below ground, despite the fact that the forced flow of air through the complex – to clear accumulations of highly explosive methane gas – would normally render the environment cool. Anyone permitted to visit the mine cannot fail to be struck by the constant hum, clatter and bustle of activity, either from the huge electrical machinery, the rapidly moving conveyor belts, or the miners and maintenance teams at work. There may be a wealth of power tools and modern machinery to ease the burden of work, but to visit the site is to see a hive of activity scarcely equalled anywhere on Earth. The work is hard and in an environment where a careless action could easily lead to an accident or worse.

The coalface is a fantastic sight; a rich seam of jet-black, glistening anthracite coal almost two metres thick and extending for a distance of 300 metres. Powerful hydraulic roof supports prevent the ever-present risk of collapse from above, while the cutter moves slowly back and forth cascading the coal on to a metal conveyor, despatching the rock on its long, long journey to the surface, the washery and ultimately the consumer. Output is of the order of 500,000 to 600,000 tons a year and the colliery's life expectancy is perhaps 10 years, extracting from the current coal seam alone. Beyond lie several other economically viable seams which remain to be exploited; there are enormous coal reserves in this area.

Unlike the Victorian era when such places were frequently operated by unscrupulous private entrepreneurs, Tower Colliery is owned by the present workforce. All 300 workers are shareholders, with a vested interest in the mine's survival and success. Tower Colliery is a place of raw humanity and good humour; a place where traditional solid values and true camaraderie remain alive, and it provides a view of an age all but past.

The coalface, Tower Colliery, Hirwaun.

METALLIFEROUS MINES

IRON

Iron has been exploited at many sites in Wales: such as Betws Garmon and Cross Foxes in the north, and at Saundersfoot and Taff's Well, in the south. As with other metal ores, iron mining dates back to pre-Roman and Roman times but it was during the sixteenth century that metal mining increased in response to technological advances developed largely by German and Dutch workers. One of the earliest and arguably the most significant text on the subject of mining was *De Re Metallica* by Georgius Agricola, a doctor practising medicine in Saxony during the sixteenth century. Agricola's works have become the most valuable and comprehensive source of information on mining, mineralogy and metallurgy of the period and the techniques featured in his books were soon adopted in mining areas across Britain.

Apart from the iron nodules (containing approximately 30% iron) found in association with the Coal Measures, a number of sites in Wales possessed larger reserves of higher-grade ore. The huge pits and extensive caverns situated in Garth Woods (ST 122825) at Taff's Well, north of Cardiff, are a good example of the scale

Iron mines, Garth Woods, Taff's Well.

Wainfelin and Tranch Iron Mine, near Pontypool.

While some areas are renowned for the mining that once took place in the locality, others are not. Indeed, some areas give little indication at all as to the presence of early underground activity. From time to time, however, civil engineering projects or road schemes may uncover significant industrial archaeological remains, and further our understanding of an area's past history. A case in point was the discovery made on the outskirts of Pontypool in the early 1990s. Whilst constructing a new bypass, during the winter of 1992-93, a mine tunnel was revealed – the Wainfelin Tranch Iron Mine – the existence of which had long been forgotten by local residents. Tunnels well over one kilometre in length were accessed and the date of 1765, chalked upon a tunnel wall some 400 metres from the surface, indicates that the mine, driven in the quest for iron ore, could be very old. It is a

THE WAINFELIN AND TRANCH IRON MINE (ST 275017)

of this type of mine development. Iron ore (haematite 50-60% iron) was worked here from at least 1565 and the last phase of mining concluded in 1940. During the final stages of activity ore was exploited at some considerable depth, although the lower reaches are now totally flooded. Another deep mine complex was located at Llanharry, near Llantrisant. This was the last iron mine to operate in Wales, production ceasing in the early 1970s.

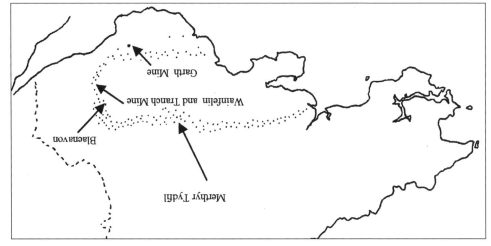

Principal Iron-ore mining areas of Wales.

IRON PYRITES/SULPHUR

In the hills to the west of Trefriw in the Conwy valley lies a little known area of mines, last worked during the Second World War. The origins of iron pyrites mining here date back hundreds of years (possibly to the Roman era) but it was not until the growth of the chemical industry in north-west England and North Wales during the 1820s that the activity expanded greatly. In large measure, this industry developed in response to the demands of the textile industries of Lancashire and Yorkshire, which utilised soaps, bleaches and dyes in the production process. The processes involved were complex but to fix the dye to particular fabrics use had to be made of chemical 'mordants', and some of these significantly altered the character and colour of the dyes themselves. One of the earliest mordants was copperas, obtained from iron pyrites, and which itself was used in the manufacture of ink and black dye. Copperas was also a source of 'oil of vitriol', or concentrated sulphuric acid, which also resulted in the production of Venetian red (an iron oxide), a highly-profitable by-product.

Scores of men would have been employed in the Trefriw mines at the end of the nineteenth century and the pyrites was largely despatched to Liverpool and Runcorn. After 1895 the Cae Coch Mine fascinating site, with all sorts of little curiosities, such as coal seams, stalactites and stalagmites and silica workings. But, given that much of the complex is potentially unstable with poor air quality, conspicuous in its location and all too inviting to the inexperienced, its entrance is gated and locked.

Cae Coch iron pyrites/sulphur mine is a superb little site, situated on the hillside behind the Roman Trefriw Wells Spa (halfway between Dolgarrog and Trefriw). The mine's main entrance – a cavernous portal – lies at the head of a steep incline. Ivy drapes over the cliff from high above and the luxuriant growth of fern gives the site something of a tropical feel. The mode of excavation adopted at this and many other mines was the 'pillar and stall' method. The pillars themselves consist of dark grey pyrites, which in its purest form contains about 47% iron and 53% sulphur. When one considers that the haematite iron ores of other areas, such as those in the vicinity of Taff's Well, contained a far higher percentage of iron, it is not difficult to understand why Cae Coch iron pyrites was processed for its sulphur rather than its iron content.

(SH 775655) was identified as an important source of sulphur for the manufacture of munitions. In 1917 some 230 people were known to be employed and by the end of the war production had risen to nearly 16,000 tons of pyrites, well over half the output for the whole of the British Isles. Work recommenced following the outbreak of the Second World War but finally ended in 1942, when bulk imports from Spain and elsewhere rendered the venture uneconomic.

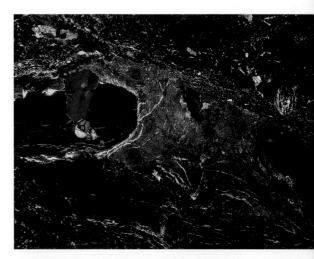

Pyrite pillar, Cae Coch Mine, Trefriw.

MANGANESE

Manganese is not common in Wales. However, deposits of this once important mineral are found in parts of North Wales, particularly in the Rhinog mountains, east of Harlech, and the Llŷn peninsula. Between Harlech and Trawsfynydd in the north, and Barmouth and Bont-ddu in the south are the remains of about 17 mines, which yielded approximately 44,000 tons. Production began in 1892 and ceased in 1928.

On the Llŷn peninsula there were two groups of mines lying within a mile of each other. The southern group included the Nant mine, near Llanfaelrhys (near Aberdaron), while the northern group included the Rhiw and Benallt mines. Ore was raised in this area from 1894 and before the last of the mines (Benallt) closed in 1945 over 196,000 tons of ore had been produced. The years of peak production were between 1905 and 1907 when output stood at over 20,000 tons a year. The ore body in Nant mine was particularly rich and yielded about 9,300 tons in 1918.

Manganese was used primarily in the iron and steel making process and in the production of manganese steel, which is hard, tough and practically non-magnetic.

LEAD AND ZINC

Deposits of lead ore have been found at sites the length and breadth of Wales. While south and north-west Wales are associated with the coalmining and slate-quarrying industries, respectively, Ceredigion and adjacent parts of Powys were once world famous for the production of silver-rich lead and zinc ore. This rurally-based industry extends back well over 3,000 years but reached its peak between 1850 and 1870. In the eighteenth and nineteenth centuries there were well over one hundred mines hereabouts. The vast majority of these were small and all have long since been abandoned. As such, the natural tranquillity of the environment has been restored but what remains is fascinating. W.G. Hoskins, the landscape historian, commented that this is

. . . perhaps the most appealing of all the industrial landscapes . . . in no way ugly but indeed possessing a profound melancholy beauty. Unlike the medieval castle with its overtones of bloodshed and war, these sites of honest endeavour as yet have few protagonists. They have been badly mauled and even destroyed in recent years regardless of archaeological merit, especially in forestry areas under the heading 'removing the scars of industry'.

Numerous old scars and spoil tips still attest to the lure of precious metal and Ordnance Survey maps of the area are dotted with former mine locations. In the Rheidol valley, near Devil's Bridge, for example, there is a deep and spectacular gorge. Here, apart from a nature reserve, are some very impressive remains of mysterious lead and silver workings. These dank mines, which are secreted within the valleys and on the hills around, should not be entered. Those curious to learn more should visit Llywernog Mine and Museum, near Ponterwyd, between Aberystwyth and Llanidloes.

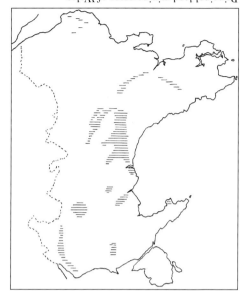

Principal lead mining areas of Wales.

Llywernog, near Ponterwyd.

Llywernog mine finally ceased operations in 1907 but the decaying complex was converted to a seven-acre 'discovery park' in the 1970s. Here the visitor will gain a good understanding of the ways in which the early miners lived and worked. There are two short, illuminated underground caverns on site, which may be explored in complete safety. The following outline of lead, silver and zinc mining in the region is graphically presented at this unique Welsh complex.

The mineral veins of this region were often thin and the valuable deposits elusive. Once the lead ore was located it would be recovered initially from small opencast workings. A simple hand windlass or perhaps a horse-powered horse-whim would be used to lift the mined material to the surface.

In time, this method of working resulted in the formation of a long trench across the

A simple hand windlass (after Agricola, *c.* 1550).

A water-driven pumping mechanism used for mine drainage.

54

ground, with perhaps occasional pillars of material left in place to hold the walls apart. But as soon as an excavation reached any depth water began to trickle into the hole and the deeper the hole was sunk the more water accumulated. This had to be removed and the normal procedure was to sink a pumping and winding shaft either in the bottom of the trench, or more usually in the rock adjacent to the mineral vein. The shaft was referred to as a winze. Where a mine was located near to a valley, an adit or drainage level might be driven horizontally into the hillside to intercept the ore vein at depth, and this approach to drainage was extremely effective, as can be seen at Llywernog. Such tunnels could be used to drain several different mine workings. The Level Fawr (SN 739723) at nearby Pont-rhyd-y-groes is a good example, being about 2.8 km (1.7 miles) in length, and from its entrance in the village it discharges water from Logau-las, Glog-fawr and Glog-fach mines.

From the bottom of the initial mine shaft horizontal tunnels or levels were slowly driven forward into the mineral-rich vein or lode. The ore was removed from the lode by the process known as stoping.

The simplest technique (overhand stoping), and most commonly employed in Wales, involved drilling shot-holes, by hand, upwards into the roof of the level and then blasting the mineral vein in order to remove the ore.

The following account, written in 1868, gives a good impression of the working conditions:

> When the lode is rich and extends upwards or downwards, it is cut away from between levels, in a regular systematic manner, strong beams being placed to support temporary platforms, on which the miners may stand and work as they ascend. When they have cut all the lode away up to the level of the lode above them, a false timber bottom is made to replace the rocky bottom of the level which is being removed. Thus, in traversing the old workings of a mine one suddenly comes to great caverns, very narrow, but of such immense height above and depth below, that the rays of your candle cannot penetrate the darkness.

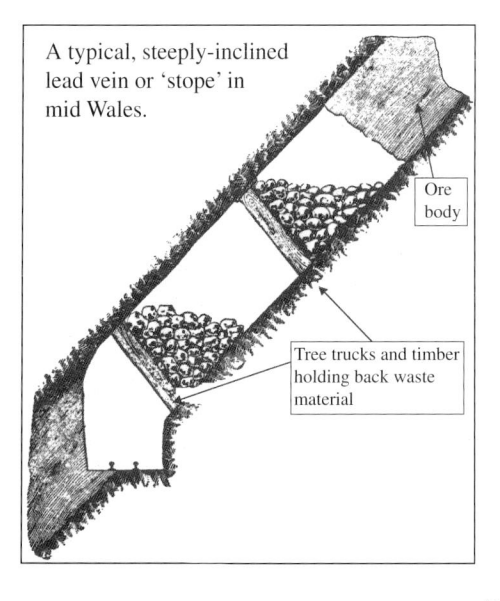

A typical, steeply-inclined lead vein or 'stope' in mid Wales.

Ore body

Tree trucks and timber holding back waste material

Working in a stope.

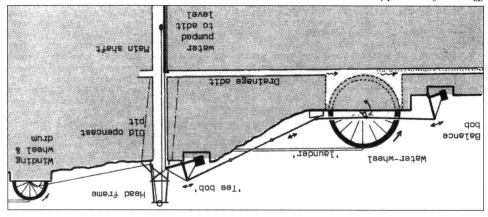

Underground waterwheel, Ystrad Einion lead mine, Cwm Einion, near Ffwrnais.

Keeping the workings free of water was a constant problem. In the coalmines and iron mines of South Wales coal-powered pumps were installed for this purpose, but in the isolated mountains of mid Wales heavy freight costs rendered the use of coal-fired steam engines uneconomic. Far cheaper was an alternative method based on the use of water wheels and a system of 'flat-rods' connected to a pump. This was a very ingenious system using a

In such places the thick, short beams that were used by the old miners are seen extending from side to side of the empty space, disappearing in dim perspective. Woe betide the man who stumbles off his narrow plank, or sets his foot on an insecure beam in such places! Where such workings are in progress, the positions of the miners appear singularly wild and insecure. The men stand in the narrow chasm between the rock walls above each others' heads, slight temporary platforms alone preserving them from certain death, and the candles of those highest above you twinkling like stars in a black sky.

normally plentiful source of renewable energy. Indeed, wherever possible, water was used to provide the power for the majority of mining operations in the area, including crushing the ore. The Llywernog complex demonstrates all of these points. However, the mountainous setting and the weather frequently conspired to make life difficult for the miners. For example, records for Llywernog show that the winters could be very hard. The year 1864 experienced an exceptionally cold start and end: in November, ice and snow stopped the pumping wheel and in December the mine flooded. The bad weather lasted until February but it was not until March 1865 that the shaft was cleared of water and work could resume. Then, just a few months later, there was a drought! Despite the use of reservoirs, shortage of water was a serious problem. In July 1867 the lower levels of the mine had to be abandoned once again: 'The water is all out of the pond, the machinery idle, and the water in the mine is nearly up to the roof . . .' When rain fell that August there was still an insufficient supply of water for crushing purposes and it was mid-September before everything was fully back in production. By 1870 water power was supplemented by the first operational use of a steam engine.

In addition to lead ore, copper, zinc blende, silver and minute traces of gold are also found. Indeed, small quantities of silver were found in almost all the lead mines of mid Wales. From the late 1730s onward metallurgical advances meant that zinc could be effectively extracted from the zinc blende, which was known as 'black jack' or 'metallic sulphur'. The primary use of this metal was for alloying with copper to form brass, but later in the 1840s the process of coating sheet iron or steel with zinc – known as galvanising – was developed.

However, no matter what mineral was sought, metalliferous mining was an occupation fraught with danger. At every stage in the operation the miner was liable to be confronted by a rock fall, water suddenly flooding into the workings, deep shafts, poor ventilation of the tunnels, and dangers posed by the heavy ore-processing equipment on the surface. The following extracts from official reports outline fatal incidents at Fron-goch (SN 723745), one of the largest mines in Cardiganshire:

16 March 1876: Richard Jones – miner, age 14

He and his father were working together in the 117 fathom level, stoping in the roof. They had newly fired a hole, and were proceeding to the spot to break away the loose [rock]. The father requested the youth to stand up on one side whilst he went up to do this, but before he had ascended much more than a yard, a piece of the loosened rock fell down and caused his son's death.

15 November 1876: Wm. Jenkins – miner, age 25

Hang fire on a gunpowder charge. Severely injured and died the next day.

15 May 1877: David Richards, dressing boy, age 14

Killed on the dressing floors of Frongoch Mine. He fell into the cog-wheel and was fatally injured.

21 November 1879: John Lewis – miner, age 27

Suffocated in sand which unexpectedly fell upon him in his working place, the 117 fathom level. This was sent down the passes from the surface to fill up worked out stopes. No sand was being tipped that day; some unexplainable obstruction had held it back.

58

Old lead workings, Cwmystwyth.

LEAD MINING AT CWMYSTWYTH
(SN 803746)

For sheer extent of surface and subterranean working Cwmystwyth has no equal and ranks as one of the oldest lead mining sites in Europe. The hillsides are scarred by steep inclines, old waterways, spoil tips and dark openings, and underground there are many kilometres of

tunnels. There is little doubt that the complex as a whole deserves some form of World Heritage or other conservation status.

While evidence has been found of lead working in the Bronze Age, possibly dating to 1800 BC, it is believed that the Romans were the first to work the site intensively. Following the Norman conquest, Cistercian monks were also involved in lead mining and the magnificent, ruined abbey of Strata Florida, to the south of Cwmystwyth, made use of considerable quantities of lead during the twelfth and thirteenth centuries. By the year 1201 this was possibly the grandest abbey in Wales and some of the fresh water conveyed to the site was supplied by a 10 cm (4 inch) diameter lead pipe. Lead was also used for the latticework around the windows and it has been calculated that some seventy tons of lead would have been required to roof the buildings alone.

After 1500 the interest in lead rose steadily. As the miners tunnelled ever deeper in their quest for ore, the problem of drainage intensified. As a result, people such as Morgan Herbert were to drive horizontal tunnels into the hillside to remove the water. Herbert's Level,

completed during the 1670s, gave access to a particularly good area of high-grade ore which resulted in the excavation of a tunnel over six metres wide and extending for almost 200 metres. During the 1760s Cwmystwyth mines reached their zenith under the direction of Thomas Bonsall, a mine manager who came from Derbyshire, an area noted for its lead mines. It was during this period, probably around 1780, that the drainage tunnel known as Level Fawr or Bonsall's Level (SN 806748) was driven. This and other horizontal tunnels excavated into the hillside made it possible to mine many of the ore bodies. The 1790s was the most profitable period of mining and in 1792, for example, some 46 tons of ore were raised per month. For his efforts Bonsall was knighted in 1796.

Level Fawr, Pont-rhyd-y-groes.

Bonsall's Level, Cwmystwyth.

Various companies and operators managed the Cwmystwyth mines over the following years. However, by the 1870s John Taylor and Sons were in considerable financial difficulty. The main reason for the failure of the mines at this time was that the best ore veins had already been worked out. However, the isolated location of the mine also posed problems, as did the wet climate which made it difficult to keep the workings dry. In addition, the mineral veins were unpredictable in both direction and ore content. By 1876 production was a disastrous 15 tons of lead per month, although elsewhere in Cardiganshire there was a general boom in mining activity. In the 1880s Cwmystwyth experienced a brief economic recovery and in 1885 the production of zinc blende amounted to about 100 tons per month.

Limited capital investment, in the form of compressed-air mechanical rock borers, was to take place in the latter half of the 1870s and again after 1900. Even so, the work remained hard and the hours were long. In 1920 it was reported that some miners still drilled their shot-holes by hand with a hammer and drilling chisel, and often in very wet conditions. Furthermore, they pushed their trams by hand along the levels and often worked in foul, fume-laden air. Production amounted to some 1,850 tons of lead ore (78% lead content) between 1900 and 1905, supplemented by 4,816 tons of zinc blende (49% zinc content). But despite these seemingly high tonnages, it appears that the mine did not pay its way. The last company officially to work the Cwmystwyth mines ceased trading in 1923. Sporadic operations on a much reduced scale continued into the 1930s but the Second World War sealed the fate of the mines; the machinery was sold off and the processes of dereliction took over.

The total output of lead ore from the Cwmystwyth mines is a matter of speculation. Estimates suggest 250,000 tons, at the very least, with perhaps 54,000 tons having been produced between 1800 to 1939. Silver was also bound up with the lead, and on the assumption that each ton of ore yielded four ounces of silver it is clear that these mines would have produced a million ounces of silver, at the very least. The total production of zinc blende, begun in the 1740s, amounted to 14,630 tons. Gold was discovered in a vein beneath Copper Hill, situated on the east side of Nant yr Onnen valley but, although the content amounted to about four to five grams per ton of ore extracted, no production figures are available. Copper was also present at several sites in the complex but it appears that it was not commercially exploited.

Sadly, much of this important site has fallen into severe decay. Latter-day mining enthusiasts have reopened many parts of the underground complex which, for many years, have been inaccessible either as a result of roof collapse or because sections were deliberately closed on grounds of safety. Access to places such as Taylor's Level, at the eastern extremity of the site, involve wading through waist-deep water but lead to over 800 metres of tunnels. Other levels, such as Alderson's Adit and Herbert's Adit in the Nant yr Onnen valley, provide cavers and mine enthusiasts with shorter, relatively dry opportunities to view truly amazing workings.

The largest underground complex at Cwmystwyth is Level Fawr, which extends for upwards of 3,500 metres, but the workings can only be accessed by experienced underground explorers. In some chambers huge beams of timber (tree trunks) up to seven metres in length support a latticework of smaller timbers, which in turn serve to support thousands of tons of waste rock. This type of support, known as a cranch, is certainly one of the finest and most spectacular examples in the

British Isles. In another section lies a very impressive 'ore bin', a gathering and storage site for the ore prior to its journey to the surface by tram.

A visit to Cwmystwyth is highly recommended, if only to gain an impression of the sheer scale of mining in the valley and the magnificent surrounding scenery. Whilst some mines, such as Cwmystwyth, had a long and chequered history, others like the

Level Fawr, Cwmystwyth.

Van Mine (SN 942876), about 12 miles north-east of Cwmystwyth were to enjoy short sharp periods of amazing prosperity. Here, in 1862, an extremely rich vein was discovered, which in places was up to 62 feet wide! More than 70,000 tons of lead and 25,000 tons of zinc blende were subsequently raised, making Van one of the most important and lucrative mines of the era in the British Isles. It was abandoned in 1892.

Ore bin, Level Fawr, Cwmystwyth.

Parc lead mine, Llanrwst.

THE LEAD MINES OF NORTH WALES

Lead mining has been undertaken across much of North Wales, especially in the area known as Gwydyr Forest, north-west of Betws-y-coed. Relatively few traces of these old workings are apparent today. However, the extent of spoil and land reclamation at places such as the Parc complex (SH 787593), 1.5 km south-west of Llanrwst, gives some indication as to the extent of subterranean activity. The origins of mining in the area are shrouded in uncertainty; it may have been undertaken as early as Roman times, but little interest was taken in the mineral reserves of the area until the seventeenth century. Lead ore was shipped from places such as Trefriw quay to the smelters in Flintshire but during the eighteenth century it appears that no more than 100 tons or so was shipped in any one year. During the nineteenth century production of various minerals expanded significantly and in time the railways came to dominate the means of transport.

The Parc complex was eventually to become the most important site in the area. In the early 1950s, for example, more ore was raised here in one month than was being raised from the whole Gwydyr Forest mining field in any one year during the nineteenth century. Operations at this mine were thoroughly modernised during and after the Second World War and in 1952 an advanced processing plant was installed. A measure of the 'expectation' that this generated can be gauged by the size of the new ore bin, the place where ore was stockpiled prior to passing through the mill. The old bin held some 60 tons, while the new one could accommodate 500 tons. It is important to remember that much of the ore stockpiled in the bin was waste material or 'gangue'. Indeed, at Parc some 90% fell into this category.

The treatment processes were numerous, and complex, but altogether more efficient than anything previously seen in any Welsh lead mine. The ore was progressively crushed, until the ore particles were reduced to less than 1/1000 inch in diameter. The material then entered 'flotation' tanks where the liquid slurry was made to froth, allowing the lead concentrate to be collected from the top of the tank. By utilising a variety of different processes the operators were able to obtain lead and zinc, separately. The ores were finally filtered, dried and bagged ready to be transported to the lead and zinc smelters based in Chester and Swansea, respectively. By 1955 over 300 tons of material a day was passing through the system. Mining ceased at Parc in 1938, although there was a brief resumption of activity in 1962, conducted by the Department of Scientific and Industrial Research.

Another important area of lead mining was to be found in north-east Wales, associated with the belt of limestone trending north to the sea from Llangollen. In the Halkyn and Minera districts lead has been extremely important to the local economy and evidence of former extensive mining activity abounds. The Newcomen 'atmospheric' pump was in use in Flintshire within a few years of its invention in 1705 and, by the early 1720s, Abraham Darby's coke smelting process, for use in the iron industry, was also being applied at Bersham in Denbighshire. It is clear that the lead mines yielded good financial returns and in the two centuries prior to 1939 one estimate gives an output of some £20 million pounds worth of minerals from the operations in Flintshire and Denbighshire.

Prior to the twentieth century, water was to prove a major obstacle to mining activity and prevented the extraction of substantial reserves of lead. The veins were particularly rich beneath Halkyn Mountain and in order to recover the

Abandoned trams, Olwyn Goch mine, Hendre.

metal ores from the deeper veins a drainage level was driven into the mountain from the coast to the north. By the time the Milwr Tunnel (SJ 222754) had reached Cadole, near Mold, it had successfully drained over 50 lead veins and created over 95 km of interconnected passageways. During the twentieth century the price of lead was falling rapidly but, despite this setback, the mining consortium was still able to reap profits from its enterprise as it gained access to many rich lead veins. Even during the depression of the 1930s the operations continued with considerable enthusiasm. Indeed, the mining company employed some 650 men at this time and several world tunnelling records were broken.

Olwyn Goch mine, situated near the upper section of the Milwr Tunnel was to be one of the more important points of access to this extensive mine complex, but there were many others. Following the closure of this lead-zinc mine in 1987 much of the surface infrastructure, including the pithead winding gear, was dismantled, but the equipment was subsequently given a new lease of life when it was re-erected at Dolaucothi gold mine. Abandoned at various points within the Olwyn Goch mine are many industrial artefacts, including five locomotives (three battery powered and two diesel), drilling machines and around 60 wagons!

GOLD

Gold-bearing rock occurs in relatively few locations. The main gold belt lies in the rugged mountainous area near Dolgellau in Gwynedd, although the precious metal was also mined at Dolaucothi in Carmarthenshire. In the Dolgellau area, gold is found in fairly well-defined mineral veins in rocks of Cambrian age (520 million years old), while the ore-bearing rocks at Dolaucothi, between Llanwrda and Lampeter, are approximately 438 million years old.

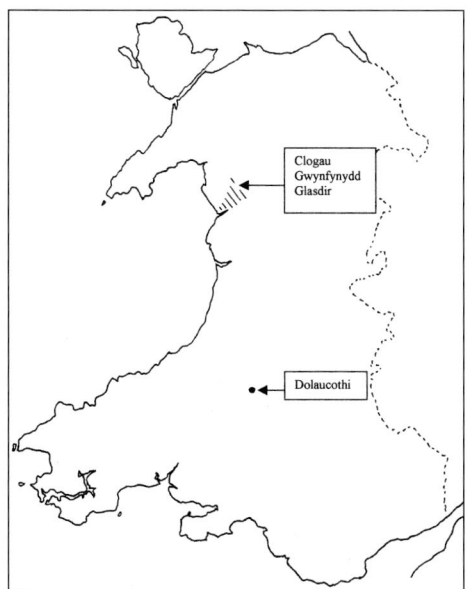

Principal gold mining area of Wales.

DOLAUCOTHI GOLD MINES (SN 670410)

Dolaucothi is the only place in Britain where the Romans are known to have mined gold. The Romans arrived in west Wales in about 75 AD, lured perhaps to this isolated area by prior knowledge of earlier mineral extraction. They established a fort at what is today the village of Pumsaint and soon began working the site in a determined manner. A good supply of water was essential, for the Romans employed controlled floods of water to recover the gold from opencast workings. This technique, known as 'hushing', first removed the covering of soil and then the mined debris. The water was brought to the site by a series of aqueducts and stored in reservoirs above the working area. In total the Romans removed over 500,000 tonnes of rock from Ogofâu Pit, a huge opencast working approximately 24 metres deep and well over 100 metres in diameter. Today the 'pit' has a relatively flat floor but in Roman times it would have been very irregular and with any number of veins leading underground. It is interesting to reflect that the total volume of gold recovered from the vast amount of excavated debris would

Dolaucothi gold mine.

probably occupy a 36 centimetre cube (less than 18 inches).

Mining by its very nature is a particularly destructive activity, one phase of development may be radically transformed or even entirely removed by succeeding phases. Nevertheless, it would appear that the majority of the tunnels accessible today would have been worked by the Romans in the first instance. For example, the two adits known as Lower and Upper Roman Levels, first described in detail in 1767, are similar in terms of their size and shape to Roman tunnels found in Spain and Romania. These were clearly hand-driven, as the surviving pick and chisel marks demonstrate.

Separating the valuable gold from the rock in which the ore is found can be problematic. The Roman operation at Dolaucothi was a fairly simple affair, for they were only concerned with recovering the so-called 'free gold'. The concentration process may well have commenced by hammering and hand-sorting the high-grade material, which was then crushed and ground manually using large pestles and mortars or rotating quern-stones similar to those used in the milling of flour. The material would then have been sieved and the fine gold would have been recovered from 'washing tables'. Given the fact that the gold was very finely distributed throughout the rock at Dolaucothi, it is likely that much of the gold mined was actually lost in the subsequent processing, but the operation was rendered profitable by virtue of the fact that much of the workforce came in the form of slave or convict labour.

Little is known about the extent of mining after the Roman period and it was not until 1844 that activity re-

Roman tunnel, Dolaucothi.

commenced once more. Relatively little gold was recovered as a result of nineteenth-century operations but during the early years of the twentieth century, James Mitchell, a Cornishman with experience in the South African gold mines, managed a profitable enterprise employing up to 12 men. For a brief period during the 1930s the deeper veins below Ogofâu Pit were exploited and at the peak of production 200 people were employed in the mine and the mill. Based upon 1995 prices, the gold recovered would have been worth about £340,000!

The ore was never particularly rich at Dolaucothi and, despite the application of considerable technology in later years, mining was intermittent and unprofitable. After 1939 the site was abandoned and most of the surface

Dolaucothi gold mines now welcome over 18,000 visitors a year.

structures were removed. The mines, originally part of an extensive estate, were given to the National Trust in the early 1940s and during the 1980s, in close liaison with Cardiff University, they began developing the site for the purposes of education and tourism. In 1988, much of the surface infrastructure of the Olwyn Goch lead-zinc mine, near Mold, was dismantled and transported to Dolaucothi. Today, therefore, the mine complex has a fine head-frame re-established over the old 1930s shaft, a fully operational winder house and a range of other mining equipment.

Situated well off the normal tourist routes, Dolaucothi gold mines welcome about 18,000 visitors a year. It is a very special place, for the National Trust have not only conserved the site but also offer underground tours and the opportunity to pan for gold! It is certainly worth a visit.

THE DOLGELLAU GOLDFIELD

Although some 150 shafts and levels are known to exist, the three main centres of activity were Gwynfynydd (SH 735275) and Glasdir (SH 741225), north of Dolgellau, and Clogau (SH 675201), about a kilometre north of Bont-ddu between Dolgellau and Barmouth. Clogau, in common with some other mines in the area, started life in the 1840s as a producer of copper but by the 1860s the lure of gold was uppermost. Mining continued here up to the Second World War; indeed, the St David's gold mine (SH 668194), a short distance above Bont-ddu, continues to attract speculators although work is

Clogau mine, near Bont-ddu.

67

Gwynfynydd gold mine, some four kilometres north of Ganllwyd, was one of the largest and most important in the area. Mining began here about 1864 and a rich strike of gold-bearing ore was made in 1895. Major operations ceased in 1938, although some work was undertaken in the late 1990s. Some of the structures remaining on the surface are of interest to the industrial archaeologist, particularly the ore concentration plant and the steel water pipes which powered a turbine.

Total output of gold is estimated to be about 80,000 ounces from the Clogau complex and about 40,000 ounces from Gwynfynydd. The yield from Glasdir is unknown but Glasdir mine, which also produced copper, is significant in the annals of mining history as it was here that William Elmore and family designed and constructed the first practical flotation plant for the separation of minerals from crushed ore. The process was to be quickly adopted world-wide and is still in use today.

Gwynfynydd gold mine, near Ganllwyd.

sporadic. From a portal driven into the banks of Afon Hirgwm, this mine extends for a considerable distance and connects with the original Clogau workings. Some deep and impressive shaft entrances may be viewed on the hill to the east of the Hirgwm valley. This area was a particularly important gold producer and yielded some 43,155 ounces between 1900 and 1905. At the height of this boom period, about 500 men were involved in mining in this district.

COPPER

Copper ores have been found in various areas across Wales, including, for example, at the head of the Neath valley, near St David's in Pembrokeshire, Cwmystwyth near Aberystwyth, on the shores of Glaslyn at the foot of Snowdon, the Great Orme at Llandudno and at Parys Mountain on Anglesey. Copper was worked from the very earliest of times. However, it was not until the metal was alloyed with tin to form bronze, hard enough for the manufacture of tools and weapons, that its use became more widespread. Copper was used to sheath the Admiralty's ships of war, in order to prevent the growth of seaweed and barnacles and to protect timber from the ravages of wood-boring worms and molluscs. Later, in the nineteenth century, it was discovered that copper could be combined with zinc to form brass, a metal extensively used during the Industrial Revolution.

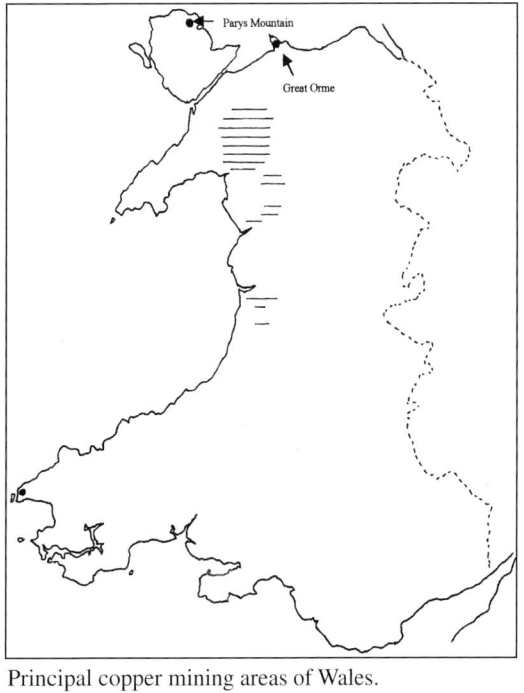

Principal copper mining areas of Wales.

GREAT ORME COPPER MINES, LLANDUDNO (SH 769831)

The discoveries at this site have necessitated a re-evaluation of the history of metalworking and prehistoric trading in western Europe. The copper ore, formerly mined on this prominent limestone headland, which also boasts a number of natural caves, is found in a series of north-south veins. The earliest activity dates back to the Stone Age and the labyrinth of painstakingly excavated tunnels, which have been unearthed over the past hundred years, are clear evidence of the efforts made by prehistoric man to obtain copper at this site. In 1832, for example, miners uncovered a section of passage containing many hundreds of artefacts. These included 'broken stags horn' and two items of bronze which were assumed to be

parts of picks. In 1849 a further discovery was made. A large, indeed cavernous, section of mine tunnel was gained where the roof and sides were 'encrusted with beautiful stalactites, to which the mineral had given beautiful hues of blue and green'. The finds on this occasion included stone hammers, weighing between 2 lb and 40 lb, and large numbers of copper-stained bones of ox, deer, goat and pig.

Another highly significant discovery was made in 1976 when an amateur archaeologist located two large galleries. Radiocarbon dating of some of the artefacts yielded a date in excess of 1020 BC. As a consequence, when Aberconwy Borough Council proposed a land reclamation scheme for the site in the late 1980s, a major investigation was initiated involving Gwynedd Archaeological Trust, together with other specialist groups. Soon after the work began, an elaborate network of subterranean workings was uncovered. The artefacts found dated back to at least 1700 or 1800 BC.

The full extent of the three to four thousand year old workings has yet to be fully established but it would appear that they covered at least five kilometres of tunnels and penetrated to a vertical depth of 70 metres. It is conservatively estimated that over 40,000 cubic metres of material

Great Orme copper mine, Llandudno.

was removed during the thousand year working period in the Bronze Age, sufficient it is thought to have yielded about 1,500 tons of metal or perhaps 10 million bronze axes! The discoveries at the Great Orme are quite unparalleled in Britain; indeed, it's a site of great international importance.

Detailed study of the excavated artefacts revealed over 900 stone objects alone. At least 90% of these could be classed as hammerstones or pounders, while the remainder are thought to have been used as crushing surfaces. The identification of mortar and pestle stones is an indicator of more thorough processing of the ore on site, rather than simple hammering. The pestles conform to a fairly standard size in that they fit easily into one hand. Their size also accords well with the hollows or depressions in the mortar stones into which they easily sit. Hammerstones were often employed as primary mining tools, perhaps where the rock vein was too hard to permit the more usual method of extraction using wood, bone or antler tools. However, 'fire-setting' is another technique that may have been used by Bronze Age people. Lighting a fire directly below or adjacent to an ore body would cause the rock to expand, and rapid cooling, with the aid of water, would lead to contraction. As a consequence, the rock would be weakened, allowing blocks to be prized free with minimal hammering. The larger stones, or pounders, may well have been reserved for crushing ore-bearing rocks after they had been removed from the vein. Many thousands of prehistoric bone tools have been found in this complex.

The passages in the mine are very constricted in places – less than 25 cm wide – suggesting that many of the miners must have been small adults or even children. Careful examination of the tunnels shows that the miners took advantage of the geology by following the softer parts of the vein, which could be removed largely by hand. Simple tools of bone, antler or wood would have been sufficient to work these areas. Harder rocks may have required the use of stone hammers or 'fire-setting'. However, it is extremely difficult to envisage the working conditions that confronted the early miners. Lying in constricted fissures deep underground, the air would soon have been rendered foul and without artificially induced ventilation it would have been difficult to keep a primitive candle alight for any significant period of time.

At present, the evidence for the use of bronze or copper tools for rock extraction is slight. However, given the precious

A constricted man-made passage, Great Orme copper mine, Llandudno. Note the bone digging tool and the stone pounder.

nature of the metal and the relatively complex series of processes required to transform the ore to metal of reasonable grade, the early miners would have been reluctant to abandon such valuable objects, broken or otherwise, unlike those implements of wood, stone or bone. It is obvious that metal tools would have been beneficial where the rock was harder.

The main use of copper at this early date was as an ingredient of bronze but once iron tools appeared during the Iron Age a decrease in the demand for copper possibly led to the abandonment of the mines. It is significant to note that no iron tools have been found in the early workings. Furthermore, there is no direct evidence for mining during the Roman period and it is possible that these mines remained unworked until they gained a new lease of life during the seventeenth century.

Fire-setting would have been a useful aid to ore extraction by this time but of greater importance, both here and throughout all mining regions, was the introduction of gunpowder. Gunpowder was introduced to British mining districts between the 1660s and 1680s, but its adoption was not common until 1700. Even as late as 1730 many old miners in neighbouring Flintshire were afraid of gunpowder and would not use it. In February 1834 an important development began, namely the driving of the Pennorfa Level, a drainage tunnel which, when completed in 1842, was about 799 metres (874 yards) in length. Even with the aid of gunpowder, projects such as this were slow and tedious; Pennorfa was excavated by 12 miners, working day and night, and their rate of progress amounted to about two metres a week! Drilling the shotholes had to be done by hand, with one miner holding and rotating the drill, while another struck it with a hammer. Setting off the explosive charge was frequently difficult and dangerous, and it was not until the 1830s that the 'safety fuse' was invented. This burned at a fairly predictable speed and was less prone to extinction or premature explosion.

Ventilation was a major concern in all mines, whether explosives were being used or not. Some elaborate systems were devised with the aim of keeping the air within the tunnels as pure as possible. Once connected with the older workings, the Penmorfa Level not only drained some 130 metres of overlying rock but also generated an invaluable through-flow of air. The new adit also allowed the miners to work below its level and in 1849 work was being undertaken between 30 and 40 metres below sea level. Not surprisingly, perhaps, the operations experienced serious problems with water.

At the height of mining operations on the Great Orme, between 1830 and 1860, some 300-400 men were employed. Each miner wore a felt or leather hat, with a wide brim which served to protect him from water dripping from the roof. For light he would use a tallow candle, which was fixed to the front of the hat with the aid of a lump of clay when climbing ladders, and then set in clay on a rock ledge near the working face. On their feet the miners wore wooden clogs and the imprint of these may still be seen in parts of the mine. At Llandudno, and in mines elsewhere, boots or clogs have occasionally been found in corners at the end of a mine tunnel, deliberately set aside by superstitious souls who hoped that by so doing good luck would accompany their efforts.

The Great Orme was only one of a group of copper mines on the mainland of North Wales, but it was by far the most successful. Some lumps of very pure ore were occasionally found but, in general, the percentage of copper within the sorted ores varied from about 3 to 34%. Much of the sorting was done as close to the site as possible but for smelting the ore had then to be shipped to works in either Lancashire, Amlwch or, particularly, Swansea, which came to dominate the field of copper smelting in the British Isles as early as the 1720s, owing to the fact that it was best sited to smelt the rich ores from Cornwall. Furthermore, coal was half the price in South Wales, so that by 1750 over half the total output of British copper was being smelted near Swansea. It is likely that ore production on the Great Orme yielded between 2,000 and 3,000 tons of copper metal, over half of which was probably obtained during the early period of mining. Such output, however, was dwarfed by the mines on Anglesey, where enormous quantities of low-grade ores were worked from the 1760s onwards.

In 1848 foreign ores, particularly those from America, Australia and Chile, became cheaper following the abolition of import duties. This was to herald the decline of Welsh copper mining and the eventual cessation of all operations in the British Isles.

Since 1991 the Great Orme mine site has been developed as a tourist attraction. However, archaeological research at the site is by no means complete and many questions require further investigation. It is known, for example, that many of the stone pounders came from further afield, which suggests an established pattern of trading. Equally intriguing is the origin of the tin ore which these early people required to mix with the copper to produce bronze, and the nature of the smelting process which entailed generating temperatures as high as 1100°C.

SYGUN COPPER MINE, BEDDGELERT (SH 605488)

Sygun Copper Mine and Elmore's flotation plant, near Beddgelert.

Sygun Copper Mine is located in the Gwynant valley, less than a mile due east of Beddgelert. As with other mines in the region, traces of gold and silver have also been found here but the principal ore worked was that of copper. Mineral extraction may well date to the Roman era, but this has yet to be proved. The mine was certainly in use by the mid 1820s and over the next five years about 500 tons of ore were produced. The ore concentrate was taken by horse and cart to Beddgelert and from there to the quay at Porthmadog, ultimately being sold for processing in Swansea. Despite modest returns, it is clear that Sygun was barely viable. Some 17 men are recorded as working the site in 1843 but by 1862 operations were suspended. Renewed activity took place in the 1880s and by the close of the century the Elmore family (associated with Glasdir mine, on the banks of the river Mawddach some miles to the south) had installed a highly innovative process to try and process the low-grade ore more effectively. Despite the investment, however, Sygun failed to make a profit. The mine finally closed in 1903 and in 1907 all the capital equipment was transported to Elmore's successful Glasdir mine, near Dolgellau.

Following several years of preparatory work, Sygun was opened as a show mine at Easter 1986. Today, the underground tour guides the visitor through various passageways before emerging at the Victoria Level after having made an ascent of just over 40 metres (140 feet) through the hillside. From this panoramic vantage point it is possible to appreciate not only the immense difficulties that confronted the miners who were required to work the site, but also the excellent interpretative centre developed by the present owners.

Sygun Copper Mine,
near Beddgelert.

An underground guided tour,
Sygun Copper Mine,
near Beddgelert.

Two miles south of Amlwch, on Anglesey, lies the gently rolling upland known as Parys Mountain. The summit skyline here is dominated by two striking structures, both of which attest to the mineral wealth lying beneath the surface. Closer inspection reveals a huge metal head-frame, so reminiscent of those once common in coalmining districts, and a large stone tower, once the site of a windmill. Between the two lies a huge opencast pit, the site of immense mineral exploitation in past years. In the 1780s, for example, the mines were to yield the highest tonnages of copper ore in the world, some 3,000 tons per annum. In 1785 the workforce was an astounding 1,500 men, women and children. Copper was worked over a vertical range of about 200 metres, the greatest depth achievable utilising the technologies of the time. Ore was first mined from shafts and levels but, subsequently, a massive collapse meant that much of the site had to be worked by opencast methods. By 1815, however, the price of copper had dropped and the best lodes had been worked out; as a consequence, production began to fall.

In July 1819 Michael Faraday visited Parys Mountain and his account paints a vivid picture of one of the mines, the hazardous nature of the working environment and the technology required to extract the ore:

We now dressed. I stripped off everything but my stockings and boots and took possession of a miners trousers, shirt and coat all of thick flannel. Then, putting on a thick woollen cap, hanging a candle to my breast button and taking another lighted and garnished with clay in my hand I was now ready to descend.

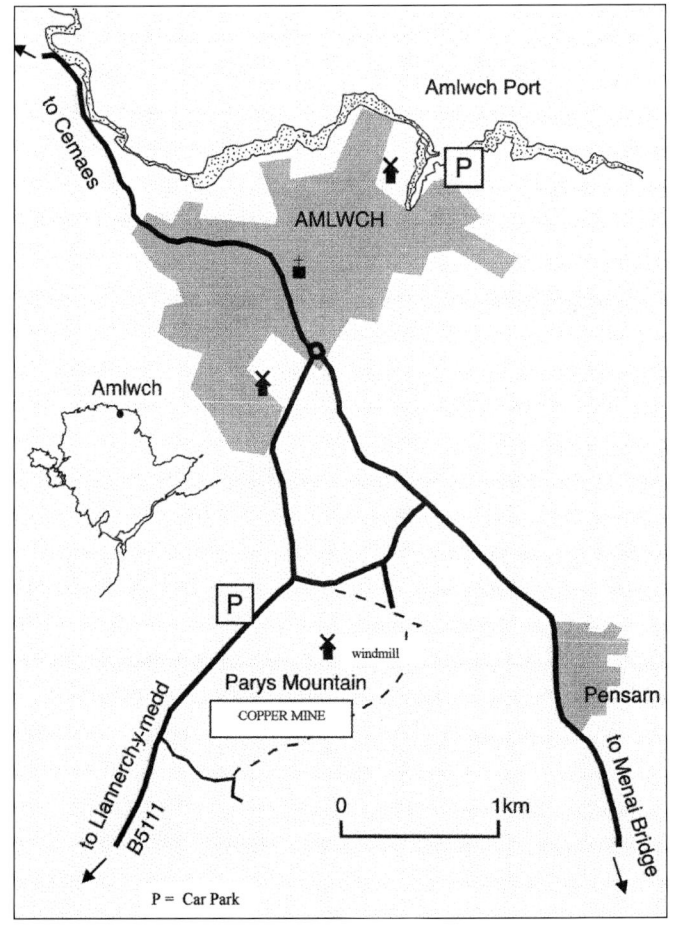

Parys Mountain, Anglesey.

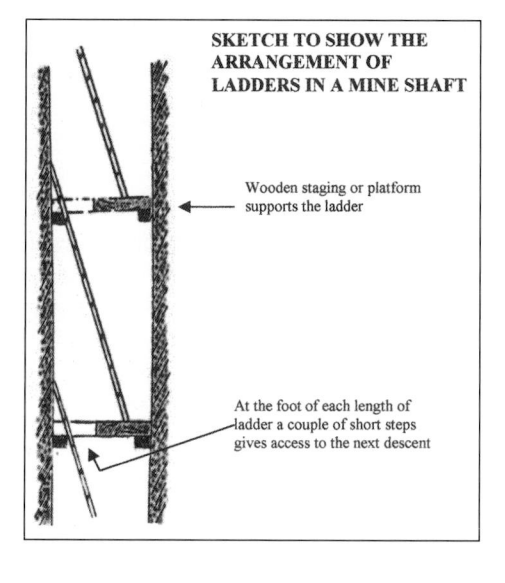

SKETCH TO SHOW THE ARRANGEMENT OF LADDERS IN A MINE SHAFT

Wooden staging or platform supports the ladder

At the foot of each length of ladder a couple of short steps gives access to the next descent

The place we prepared to descend was a small aperture in the earth about 4 feet by 3 feet wide and a ladder appeared at its mouth which descended into the darkness below. Captain Leaman chose this shaft because it was the most comfortable. There were two others but the pump rods worked up and down in one and in the other we could only ascend and descend in the buckets like lumps of ore. A fall would have led us down 200 or 300 feet without any ceremony or hesitation . . . Our progress in the vein was at first through very confined passages but on a sudden we entered a place like a large chamber so large that our light would not reach across it . . . Here again it became very narrow and we had in one corner to lay down on our backs and wriggle in through a rough slanting opening not more than 12 or 14 inches wide.

Proceeding along one of these galleries we came at last to a chasm at the bottom of which we could just see men with lights . . . Now at times we began to hear explosions which reverberated throughout the mine in grand style and we soon came up to two men who were preparing a blast. A hole is cut first by chisels in the rock in the direction thought most proper and from 12 to 24 inches deep according to circumstances. This being cleaned out by proper tools a portion of gunpowder is placed in the bottom of it and then a long thin iron rod called a needle being put down into the gunpowder, pounded stone is introduced and rammed hard with an iron tool on to the gunpowder. More stone is introduced until the hole is full and then the needle being withdrawn, a straw filled with powder or sometimes quills so filled are put down the hole and make a communication with the charge below. A bit of touch paper is then attached to the external gunpowder and being lighted the men retire a few yards off round some projection or corner whilst the explosion happens. When it has taken place the ore or stone thrown off is removed and the process again repeated. It is astonishing how careless the men become of the peculiar dangers to which they are liable from the frequency with which they meet them. They go on hammering without the least care at the hole charged with powder and now and then explode it by the attrition they cause before they are out of the way and then men get killed. They put their candles anyhow and anywhere and their powder is treated in the same manner. Magrath, to rest himself whilst the Captain gave directions, sat down on a tub and stuck his candle against its side. We found out afterwards it was what they kept the powder in and it certainly would not have been wonderful if we had all made a grand blast together.

Following the example of the Captain and peeping into a small chasm through which a man might by contrivance pass, we found it to be the entrance into a large cavity from 30 to 40 feet wide every way. This had been a fine bunch of ore and there were 6 or 7

men with their candles working in it. We did not go down but putting our lights aside laid our heads to the aperture and viewed this admirable Cimmerian scene for some time with great pleasure, the continual explosion on all sides increasing the effect. This was the lowest part of those workings and was about 370 feet below the surface of the earth.

After a little further progress we came to the pump shaft, an aperture cut down from the surface to this spot. It was 360 ft. deep and we could see no daylight up it. Below it was a small well and into this were inserted pumps. The first was a lifting pump and raised the water a few feet. Then a forcing pump took it and made it ascend up pipes far away out of sight. The pumps were worked by the steam engine we had seen above (on the surface) being connected with it by means of wood descending in the shaft and continually rattling up and down in it. In the small part of the shaft left vacant by the pistons pipes and beams were fixed ladders which ascending from stage to stage conducting to the top and up. There we had to go bathed in the shower of water which was shaken off from all parts of the pump works. After long climbing we came to a part of the shaft where the first forcing pump delivered its water into a little cistern and then another pump of the same

Old underground workings, Parys Mountain copper mines, near Amlwch.

The modern entrance to Parys Mountain copper mines.

construction threw it up to the surface. Still proceeding we at last got a glimpse of daylight above and were soon able to see the pump rods by it. Now the danger of the ascent appeared far greater than before for the more extensive light showing in the well above and something of the depth below made us conscious of our real situation whereas before we only thought of the small spot illuminated by our candles. The agitation of the pump rods was more visible too and appeared greater from being seen over a larger space and their rattling and thumping was quite in accordance with appearances. But in spite of all things we gained the surface in high glee and came up into the world above at the engine after a residence of about two hours in the queer place below.

Periodic mining revivals took place on Parys Mountain up until 1883, when it appears that large-scale operations finally ceased. Small-scale excavation continued into the early years of the twentieth century but thereafter the site was abandoned. During the 1960s and 1970s interest in the site was rekindled and there followed an extensive programme of drilling and evaluation. In the 1980s a major new ore body was discovered about 1 kilometre west of the old workings and between 1988 and 1990 a shaft, whose head-frame provides the most conspicuous landmark in north Anglesey, was sunk to a depth of 300 metres. Subsequently, about 1,000 metres of side tunnel was driven at a depth of 280 metres. Further study by Anglesey Mining Company plc has revealed a significant resource of base metal amounting to about 6.5 million tonnes. Approximately 2,000 tonnes of ore were successfully hoisted and processed through a pilot plant constructed on site and about 200 tonnes of ore concentrate were sold to the smelter at Avonmouth. The metal content was approximately 5.3% zinc, 2.3% copper, 2.7% lead, 39 grams of silver and 0.32 grams of gold per tonne. It would appear that the reserves of ore cover an area measuring 3 km by 1.5 km and planning permission has been obtained to develop a 1,000 tonne per day mine. However, declining metal prices and weakening stock markets in the early 1990s resulted in the mine development being placed on hold. Thanks to the Marquis of Anglesey and Anglesey Mining plc some areas of the old mine have been reopened for recreational visits by cavers and other specialist mining groups. The principal activists in the area,

Opposite: The old windmill and modern head-frame (right), Parys Mountain, near Amlwch.

the Parys Underground Group, have so far charted approximately 2.5 km of underground passages, dating mainly to the eighteenth and nineteenth centuries. The passages cover a vertical range of 27 metres (90 feet) and many interesting archaeological discoveries have been made. Perhaps the most fascinating is that of a Bronze Age bell pit – initially uncovered by Victorian miners – and a quantity of rounded stone pounders similar in appearance to those found in the Great Orme complex. At the time of publication this site awaits detailed archaeological study.

Although members of the public are unable to venture underground, an industrial heritage trail has been established on the surface, which provides a fascinating insight into the area. However, as with all mine sites, visitors are kindly reminded that places such as the Great Opencast are potentially hazardous and care is required when following the paths.

The Great Opencast, Parys Mountain copper mines, with the old windmill in the distance.

Opposite: Dinas silica mine, Pontneddfechan.

SILICA

High on the hillside above the village of Pontneddfechan, at the head of the Vale of Neath, lie a number of interconnecting openings of man-made origin. The Dinas silica mine (SN 917080) lies at the head of a spectacular section of the Sychryd gorge and is particularly interesting in that it is one of a very few Welsh stone mines. Today, very little remains as testimony to its former importance; the surface structures have long since disappeared and the tramways have grassed over. But during its heyday, in the first half of the twentieth century, the mine employed scores of men who were engaged in extracting the silica-rich sandstone for the manufacture of refractory bricks. Many of the bricks were used to line the furnaces in the Neath valley, but large quantities were also exported to several countries overseas.

The miners pursued a narrow band of rock, less than three metres thick, gently inclined towards the south. Given the inherent strength of the rock, the work was relatively safe compared to that in the coalmines just a short distance away. Even so, a similar method of extraction was employed. The miners adopted the pillar and stall technique; as they moved forward they took all the sandstone that they possibly could, leaving pillars here and there to support the overlying strata. Extraction of the silica began in the late 1700s and the mine was abandoned in 1964.

There are a number of old silica mines in this locality but the most extensive, on the north bank of the Sychryd gorge, runs into the hillside in an easterly direction for over 300 metres. Over this distance there are many parallel, interconnecting passageways. The deeper levels, below the level of the river, are completely flooded and experienced cave divers have explored this area to a depth of 22 metres.

It is known that one of the old mines contains some unusual dripstone deposits. The blue coloration on a calcite flow indicates the presence of copper (sulphate) deposits in the locality. This particular mine level was rediscovered in 1987 and although worked for silica for much of its life it may originally been opened in the quest for copper. Sadly, the blue staining has been despoiled; an exquisite sight lost forever.

Underwater exploration of the Dinas silica mines, Pontneddfechan.

Copper-stained calcite flow, Dinas silica mine, Pontneddfechan.

SLATE

In the mountains of Gwynedd it was slate that became the much sought after commodity. The rock had been worked from earliest times in a piecemeal fashion, but as the Industrial Revolution gained momentum in the later eighteenth century so, too, was there a greatly increased demand for good quality slate to roof the hundreds and thousands of new houses under construction. Slate came to dominate the economy of north-west Wales and by the mid 1800s it accounted for almost half the total revenue from trade and industry. Indeed, in Wales as a whole, its output value was comparable to that of coal. While Cardiff and Newport in the south grew in response to coal, so Bangor and Caernarfon in the north gained their prosperity from slate. Other towns such as Bethesda, Llanberis, Blaenau Ffestiniog and Porthmadog, and countless smaller communities, owed their existence to the industry.

Welsh slate is a metamorphic rock which may be split along so-called cleavage planes. By so doing it is possible to produce relatively thin sheets of material of uniform strength. Good quality slate is also impervious to water, extremely durable and may be 'dressed' and finished on the same site as its extraction. However, although universally recognised as a roofing material, almost half the tonnage produced during the nineteenth century was in the form of slabs, widely used for window and door lintels and sills, fireplaces, floors and building stones. It was also used in the manufacture of billiard tables, providing the slabs in dairies and larders, for coffins, in the lining of gents toilets, and even in the electrical field for switchboards. Much of the older purple slate of north-west Wales, formed of muds laid down in the sea over 500 million years ago, was worked in open quarries such as the Penrhyn quarry, Bethesda, and the Dinorwig quarry, Llanberis. However, a great deal of the younger grey slate, formed of muds laid down in the sea about 450 million years ago, was worked in slate mines, such as those in the vicinity of Blaenau Ffestiniog and some in the Corris area.

The general public may visit a number of old slate mines in north-west Wales. At Corris, between Machynlleth and Dolgellau, King Arthur's Labyrinth provides a walk of a quarter of a mile

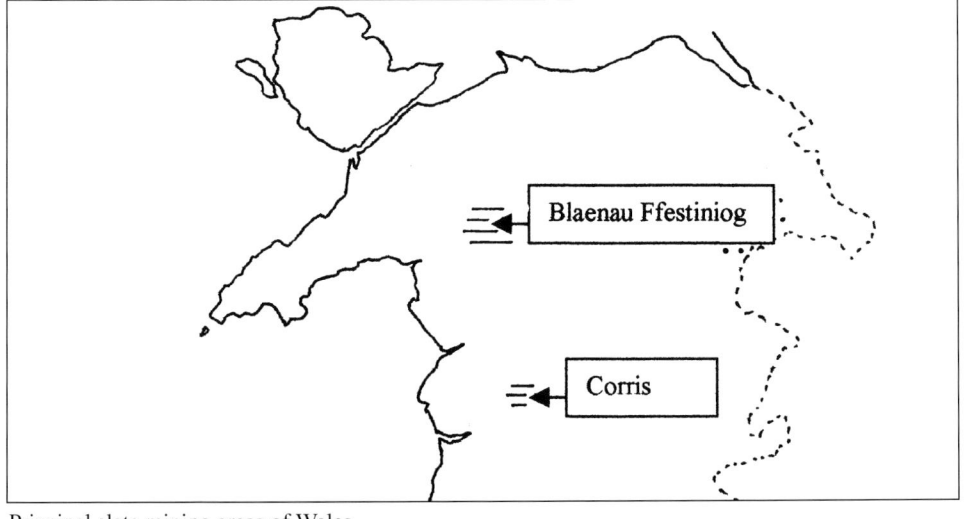

Principal slate mining areas of Wales.

Underground chamber, Rhosydd quarry, near Blaenau Ffestiniog.

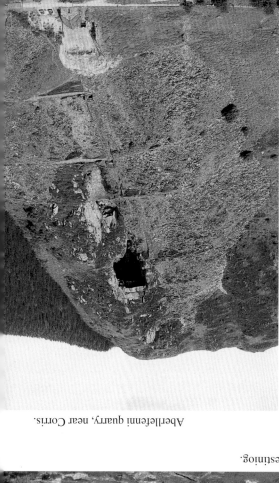

Aberllefenni quarry, near Corris.

through long abandoned slate workings, while Llanfair Slate Caverns, on the main coast road just south of Harlech, also offer an insight into the slate mining industry. Llanfair quarry was worked between 1873 and 1906 and opened to the public in 1973. The normal tour here is self-guided and takes in some large and spectacular chambers. There are some breathtaking panoramic views of Cardigan Bay from the site.

More than any other town in the British Isles, Blaenau Ffestiniog bears testimony to the importance of the slate industry. Blaenau was, in a very real sense, the main centre of the underground slate mining industry. The hillsides here are literally covered in blue-grey rock waste, vast acreages of unconsolidated reject material generated by an industry that produced about 10 tons of waste for every ton of the finished product. But the extensive underground networks and huge caverns from which much of this rock originated are hidden from sight.

85

It was not until 1755 that any significant interest was taken in the production of slate at this locality. At this time, the name Blaenau Ffestiniog simply referred to a group of cliffs several miles north of the village of Ffestiniog. Yet 100 years later it was a thriving town. At the height of the boom, prior to the First World War, many thousands of men worked in the industry, although not all were engaged underground. Often, as in the case of major quarries such as Llechwedd, an equal if not greater number were employed on the surface, manufacturing roofing slates and slabs from the blocks raised from the underground chambers. By the end of the nineteenth century an industry 'standard' had been established and slates of various sizes and weights were referred to as Empresses, Princesses, Small Duchesses, Wide Ladies and Narrow Ladies. Such slates were produced by the million and exported from local ports, particularly Porthmadog, to all parts of the world.

Splitting slate, Llechwedd Caverns, Blaenau Ffestiniog.

Underground chamber, Aberllefenni quarry, near Corris.

At its peak in 1904 Llechwedd quarry employed 639 men. As in any mine during the Victorian era conditions were hard: the working day was over ten and a half hours long in summer (shorter in winter) and the men toiled six days a week. During the winter much of the labour force would not see the sun at all. Furthermore, the temperature underground was a cool 10°C, there were often strong draughts and the workings were frequently wet. Underground lighting was woefully inadequate and well into the twentieth century this consisted of a glimmering candle stuck into a piece of clay. As the men had to pay for the candles themselves, they were sparing in their use. Later, crude lanterns were constructed by placing a candle into a discarded one-gallon oil container. It was not until the 1950s that the Oldham electric cap-lamp finally replaced the candle.

Such was the working environment that accidents were common. For example, some 21 deaths were recorded at Cwmorthin quarry (SH 681459) between 1875 and 1893, out of a workforce of about 550. In the adjoining Oakeley quarries there were 61 deaths over the same period, out of a workforce of 1,652. In the same period, Llechwedd lost 9 men and Votty and Bowydd 11. Falls from exposed, elevated positions, unexpected localised rockfalls and incidents involving machinery figure prominently among the causes of death. An extract from the report of the 1895 Parliamentary Inquiry into the industry refers to three fatalities at Cwmorthin during 1884:

A miner and 'repairer' was killed while building an underground bridge. He was moving a baulk of timber when he slipped and fell into the chamber below.

A miner was prising off a piece from the underneath of a loose dangerous roof, standing under it himself when a part of it fell on him.

A rockman was killed by an unexpected fall of slate from the forebreast. He and his partner had examined the place several times and thought that it was safe; but a large block of slate slipped away from a concealed joint and struck him in its fall. He died 16 days after the accident.

By the closing years of the nineteenth century the demand for Welsh slate had already begun to fall; imports were gaining ground and alternative, cheaper methods had been found to produce durable roofing materials. But the industry was also paying the price for failing to modernise. Pneumatic power drills, for example, were very slow to be adopted; even as late as the 1930s some managers were expressing severe reservations about their use. The tediously slow technique of using a *jwmpar* – a long metal bar – to drive the holes by hand persisted well beyond the time when logic should have rendered its use obsolete. It was the same story with wire saws to cut the slate and also with regard to the use of power in the quarries. Even as late as 1930 quarries such as Cwt y Bugail and Rhosydd (SH 664461) among many others, were without electric power. It was not until the 1950s that electric became universally available.

The first half of the twentieth century witnessed a massive decline in the industry, but since then modernisation and reappraisal of the global situation have led to a minor but significant upturn in fortunes. Furthermore, operations such as Llechwedd Slate Caverns have supplemented their declining income by becoming a major tourist attraction.

LLECHWEDD SLATE CAVERNS (SH 708471)

Llechwedd Slate Caverns became a show mine in 1972 and since that time the site has received over six million visitors. Two sections of the complex have been developed for public viewing. 'The Miners' Tramway' involves a train journey along a level tunnel for several hundred metres into the mountainside. Clattering through the darkness in a small, open-sided carriage provides a most unusual experience. A brief view of the outside world, through a 'window' in the tunnel wall reveals a huge open-air pit which marks a later phase of slate extraction at the site, but the highlights of the tour are the enormous caverns deep within the hillside. Several of these underground 'quarries' are encountered in the course of the excursion.

'The Deep Mine' is a separate tour option at Llechwedd, and is claimed to be Britain's steepest passenger railway. Here visitors travel in a specially constructed 24-seater car, which descends a gradient of 1:1.8. Disembarking from the carriage 30 metres (99 feet) below there follows a circular tour lasting approximately 25 minutes, returning the visitor to the steeply-inclined railway line at a depth of

The Miners' Tramway, Llechwedd Caverns, near Blaenau Ffestiniog.

40 metres. The tour, opened in 1979, also includes a spectacular *son et lumière*. No one can fail to be impressed by the immensity of the man-made caverns and the incredible complexity of the various levels, stacked one above the other. This is without doubt one of Europe's premier tourist attractions, as the numerous awards confirm.

'The Deep Mine' excursion, Llechwedd Caverns.

Llechwedd Slate Caverns, Blaenau Ffestiniog.

Cwt y Bugail Quarry (SH 734468)

It is a strenuous three kilometre walk to Cwt y Bugail quarry, situated east of Blaenau Ffestiniog and some 300 metres above Cwm Penmachno, but the energetic hillwalker is rewarded with a wonderful insight into the development of slate quarrying in the area. At Cwt y Bugail one can trace the various stages of quarry and mine development, and begin to understand the process of slate extraction. The industrial archaeologist and the simply curious will also marvel at the sights *en route*, and it will be a rare person who will not feel for the slate miners and the hardships they had to endure, living and working in such a harsh environment. Slate mining ceased here in the early 1970s.

Cwt y Bugail quarry, near Penmachno.

Dinorwig Hydro-electric Power Station – 'Electric Mountain' (SH 587600)

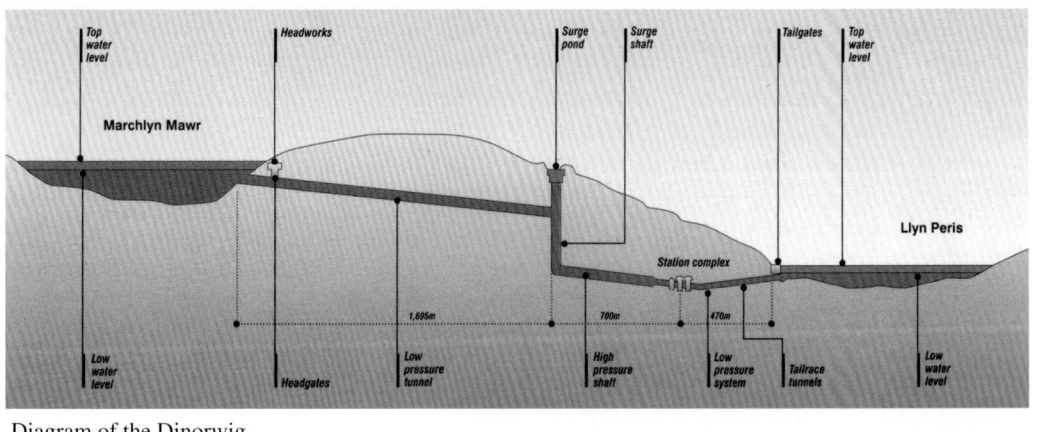

Top water level — Headworks — Surge pond — Surge shaft — Tailgates — Top water level

Marchlyn Mawr

Llyn Peris

Station complex

1,695m — 700m — 470m

Low water level — Headgates — Low pressure tunnel — High pressure shaft — Low pressure system — Tailrace tunnels — Low water level

Diagram of the Dinorwig
hydro-electric scheme.

Holyhead
Anglesey
Conwy
Llandudno
Liverpool
M53
M56
Bangor
Colwyn Bay
A55
A55
Chester
A5
B4366 A5 NORTH WALES
Caernarfon
Llanberis
Snowdon ● Betws-y-coed
A5
Wrexham
Beddgelert
Nefyn
Criccieth ● Porthmadog
Bala
Llangollen
Pwllheli
Oswestry

No book outlining the wonders of subterranean Wales could overlook the spectacular Dinorwig Power Station at Llanberis, a site which welcomes visitors and provides tours of this amazing complex.

The concept of a hydro-electric power station, generating power for domestic and industrial use, may be fairly basic, but at Dinorwig this has been taken one giant step further. Here, the water which powers the turbines is pumped back to the upper storage reservoir – Marchlyn Mawr – by night, a refilling, refuelling process powered by 'off-peak' electricity. Water is then released at times of peak demand, when the price of electricity is at its highest, and sold again to the wholesale market. Most conventional power stations produce power at a uniform rate, day and night and, as such, they are unable to respond quickly to any surge in demand. Dinorwig, however, is capable of 'instant' power generation.

The scale of the operation and statistics of the scheme are quite mind boggling. Consider, for example, that some 1,800 megawatts of electricity can be supplied 'instantly', sufficient to satisfy the whole of Wales for up to five hours. Like a sleeping giant, Dinorwig can respond almost instantly to the extra power demands from the electricity network. The station is very flexible and the plant has five basic ways of operating. For example, from zero power production to maximum output takes just 100 seconds, while in 'tick over' mode it takes just 12 seconds to generate over 1,500 megawatts. In 90 minutes more water passes down the main shaft inside the mountain than that used by London in a day. Indeed, so much water passes through the subterranean network at full operation that the upper reservoir, which holds seven

Dinorwig Hydro-electric Power Station on the shores of Llyn Peris, Llanberis.

million cubic metres of water (1,540 million gallons), rises and falls by 34 metres. Llyn Peris, 800 metres below Marchlyn Mawr, also had to be enlarged to accommodate the huge and fluctuating volume of water.

The scheme took some 10 years to reach fruition and, at a cost of £425 million, was the largest civil engineering project ever undertaken in the British Isles. This is the largest pumped-storage system in Europe and about 3,500 workers were employed in its construction, over 70% of which were drawn from the local labour force. The design was imaginative and sensitive, involving the hiding of most of the power station deep beneath the summit of Elidir Fawr. There is little doubt that the project as a whole has not only removed some of the scars of previous quarrying activity, but has also added considerably to the tourist attractions of the area. Some 16 kilometres (10 miles) of underground tunnel were constructed and one cavern is large enough to accommodate St Paul's Cathedral, London. As the visitor passes through the spacious portal and into the underground network on a bus, the sheer magnitude of the undertaking is over-whelming. Deep inside the mountain, in well lit, concrete-sprayed tunnels, one is transported some 60 metres below the level of Llyn Peris. Here the visitor may view the largest man-made cavern in Europe, 179 metres long, 24 metres wide and 60 metres high, equipped with six giant generators, each weighing 438 tons.

Owned and operated by Edison Mission Energy, Dinorwig was officially opened by the Prince of Wales on 9 May 1984. The power station is a spectacular triumph technologically and environmentally, for despite its immensity the plant itself is virtually invisible to all but the very observant. This is a site that no visitor to North Wales should miss.

CONCLUSION

There are many unique and intriguing sights to be seen in the underworld. I hope that the images presented in this book have stirred the imagination, and inspired some to share with me the wonder, the inspiration, and perhaps occasionally even the dread that this hidden world evokes. Although a great many sites are beyond the reach of the general public, cave and mine exploration is an interesting, peace-loving activity, as valid as any other recreational pursuit. And while on the one hand I hope that I have, in some small measure, communicated the enchantment of these places, I also hope that this account will help to promote the need for their long-term conservation. Conservation begins with education and awareness and the various show-caves and mines scattered across Wales are of immense value in this respect. Heritage tourism is now a thriving part of Welsh life and as it develops so, too, will our understanding and appreciation of underground Wales.

Dinorwig Hydro-electric Power Station: construction of the largest man-made cavern in Europe.

Appendix 1: Underground sites accessible to the general public:

Big Pit, The National Mining Museum of
Wales, Blaenavon, Torfaen NP4 9XP
Tel. 01495 790311
Coalmine

Dan yr Ogof, The National Showcaves
Centre for Wales
Aber-craf, Powys SA9 1GJ
Tel. 01639 730284/730801
Fax: 01639 730293
www.showcaves.co.uk
Natural cave systems

Dinorwig Hydro-electric Power Station –
'Electric Mountain'
Llanberis, Gwynedd LL55 4UR
Tel: 01286 870636
www.fhc.co.uk
Underground power station

Dolaucothi Gold Mine, Pumsaint,
Carmarthenshire SA19 8US
Tel. 01558 650707
www.nationaltrust.org.uk
e-mail: gdoest@smpt.ntrust.org.uk
Gold mine

Great Orme Mines, Llandudno, Conwy
LL30 2XG
Tel. 01492 870447
www.greatorme.freeserve.co.uk
e-mail: gomines@greatorme.freeserve.co.uk
Copper mine

King Arthur's Labyrinth, Corris,
Machynlleth, Gwynedd SY20 9RF
Tel: 01654 761584
e-mail: king.arthurs.labyrinth@corris-
wales.co.uk
Slate quarry

Llanfair Slate Caverns, Nr. Harlech,
Gwynedd LL46 2SA
Tel: 01766 780247
www.lokalink.co.uk/harlech/slatecaverns
e-mail: owen@llanfairslate.fsnet.co.uk
Slate quarry

Llechwedd Slate Caverns, Blaenau
Ffestiniog, Gwynedd LL41 3NB
Tel. 01766 830306
Fax: 01766 831260
www.welsh-slate.com
e-mail: llechwedd@aol.com
Slate quarry

Llywernog Mine and Museum, Ponterwyd,
Ceredigion SY23 3AB
Tel. 01970 890620
Fax: 01545 570823
e-mail: silverrivermine@cs.com
Lead, silver and zinc mine

Sygun Copper Mine, Beddgelert,
Gwynedd LL55 4NE
Tel. 01766 510100
Fax: 01766 510102
www.ourworld.compuserve.com
email: snowdoniamine@compuserve.com
Copper mine

Appendix 2: A few words of advice

Caves and mines are dangerous places and many cave and mine entrances lie on private land. In such cases, the visitor has no right of access or entry. Many of the sites described are remote. Remember, too, that old ruins are often unsafe to approach or enter, and that shafts may be unfenced. So, please take care. Levels or adits may appear inviting but these should not be entered.

Conservation of the underground environment is extremely important: we should leave no rubbish, nor should we cause any damage. Think of those who may wish to visit the site in the future.

Guidelines for individuals/groups wishing to explore caves and old mines have been drafted by the National Caving Association (NCA) and the National Association of Mining History Organisations (NAMHO), respectively.

Useful addresses

Association for Industrial Archaeology: The Wharfage, Ironbridge, Telford, Shropshire TF8 7AW

Historical Metallurgy Society: Rock House, Bowen's Hill, Coleford, Gloucestershire GL16 8DH

National Association of Mining History Organisations NAMHO, c/o Peak District Mining Museum, The Pavilion, Matlock Bath, Derbyshire DE4 3NR

National Caving Association (NCA): Monomark House, 27 Old Gloucester Road, London WC1 3XX

Northern Mine Research Society: 41 Windsor Walk, South Anston, Sheffield S31 7EL

UK Journal of Mines & Minerals: 3 Oak Tree Road, Bawtry, Nr Doncaster, South Yorkshire DN10 6LD

Welsh Mines Society: 20 Lutterburn Street, Ugborough, Ivybridge, Devon PL21 0NG

Appendix 3: Bibliography

Annels, Alwyn (ed.), 1995. *Dolaucothi Gold Mines*, University of Wales

Bennet, J. & Vernon R., 1989. *Mines of the Gwydyr Forest* (parts 1-7), Gwydyr Mines Publications

Bick, D.E., 1974. *The Old Metal Mines of Mid-Wales* (parts 1-6), The Pound House

Bird, R.H., 1974. *Britain's Old Metal Mines*, Bradford Barton

Bird, R.H., 1977. *Yesterday's Golcondas*, Moorland Publishing Company

Booth, A.J., 1995. *Small Mines of South Wales*, Industrial Railway Society

Carr, T. & Schone, Anne Marie, 1993. *Pigs & Ingots: The Lead/Silver Mines of Cardiganshire*, Y Lolfa

Cossons, N., 1987. *The BP Book of Industrial Archaeology*, David & Charles

Edison Mission Energy, 1999. *Dinorwig – The Electric Mountain*, Edison Mission Energy

Ebbs, C., 1993. *The Milwr Tunnel: Bagillt to Loggerheads 1897-1987*,

Farr, M., 1997. *Darkworld: The Secrets of Llangattock Mountain*, Gomer Press

Farr, M., 1999. *Dan yr Ogof: The Jewel of Welsh Caves*, Gomer Press

Farr, M., 1998. *The Secret World of Porth yr Ogof*, Gomer Press

Hall, G.W., 1971. *Metal Mines of Southern Wales*, Hall

Hall, G.W., 1988. *The Gold Mines of Merioneth*, Griffin Publications

Hughes, S.J., 1981. *The Cwmystwyth Mines*, Northern Mines Research Society

Isherwood, G., 1995. *Cwmorthin Slate Quarry*, Adit Publications

North, F.J., 1962. *Mining for Metals in Wales*, National Museum of Wales

Rees, D.M., 1975. *Industrial Archaeology of Wales*, David & Charles

Richards, A.J., 1995. *Slate Quarrying in Wales*, Gwasg Carreg Gwalch

Stratford, T., 1995. *Caves of South Wales*, Cordee

Thomas, D., 1973. *Michael Farraday in Wales*, Gwasg Gee

Thomas, T.M., 1961. *The Mineral Wealth of Wales and its Exploitation*, Oliver & Boyd

Williams, C.J., 1995. 'Great Orme Mines', *British Mining*, No. 52